Managed Care & Privatization Child Welfare Tracking Project

1998 STATE AND COUNTY SURVEY RESULTS

Charlotte McCullough & Barbara Schmitt

CWLA Press • Washington, DC

CWLA Press is an imprint of the Child Welfare League of America. The Child Welfare League of America (CWLA), the nation's oldest and largest membership-based child welfare organization, is committed to engaging all Americans in promoting the well-being of children and protecting every child from harm.

© 1999 by the Child Welfare League of America, Inc. All rights reserved. Neither this book nor any part may be reproduced or transmitted in any form or by any means, electronic or mechanical, including photocopying, microfilming, and recording, or by any information storage and retrieval system, without permission in writing from the publisher. For information on this or other CWLA publications, contact the CWLA Publications Department at the address below.

CHILD WELFARE LEAGUE OF AMERICA, INC.
440 First Street, NW, Third Floor, Washington, DC 20001-2085
E-mail: books@cwla.org

CURRENT PRINTING (last digit)
10 9 8 7 6 5 4 3 2 1

Cover design by Luke Johnson

Printed in the United States of America

ISBN # 0–87868-773-4

Contents

Acknowledgments v

Executive Summary 1

Background and Methodology 9

Principal Findings 13

Conclusions and Commentary 39

1998 State Profiles: Managed Care and Privatization Initiatives 53

Tables

Table 1. States and Localities with One or More Managed
 Care Initiatives 12

Table 2. Number of Initiatives Reporting Managed Care or
 Privatization Approaches to the Management, Finance,
 or Delivery of Child Welfare Services 14

Table 3. Size of the Initiatives 17

Table 4. Services Included in the Initiatives 18

Table 5. Quality Requirements and Outcomes Measures 22

Table 6. Methods Used to Gather Outcome and Quality Information . 22

Table 7. Contributing Agencies and Funding Streams 35

Table 8. Number of Initiatives That Report Legislative or Regulatory
 Changes 36

Table 9. The 29 States at a Glance 47

For More Information 151

References 153

iii

Acknowledgments

CWLA would like to express our great appreciation to the staff, faculty, and consultants at the National Technical Assistance Center for Children's Mental Health at the Georgetown University Child Development Center, the Human Service Collaborative, and the Research and Training Center for Children's Mental Health at the University of South Florida Louis de la Parte Florida Mental Health Institute for their ongoing coordination with us in tracking children's services and behavioral health managed care initiatives throughout the country.

EXECUTIVE SUMMARY

The Child Welfare League of America (CWLA) is a membership association of nearly 1,000 public and nonprofit child welfare agencies. Each year since 1996, the CWLA Managed Care Institute's Tracking Project has attempted to determine the extent to which public state or local child welfare agencies are applying managed care tools or privatization strategies to child welfare services. Managed care or privatization approaches can change how child welfare services are managed, how they are reimbursed, and how they are organized and delivered. In investigating the states' initiatives, The Tracking Project has posed the following questions:

- What are the broad goals of the initiative?
- What population is to be covered by the initiative?
- What services and supports will be included in the plan? What services will be provided outside the plan?
- How will quality be ensured and outcomes defined and measured under the plan?
- How will public and private management roles change?
- How will the plan be funded and how will risks be shared?

BACKGROUND/METHODOLOGY

From August 1998 to January 1999, the CWLA Managed Care Institute surveyed all state child welfare administrators or their designees, asking contacts in county-administered states to report on broad state efforts and to provide up to five county contacts who could contribute additional information on any county-specific initiatives. Results were then confirmed and narrative state profiles approved by respondents. In some instances, data from the survey were supplemented with additional information from public documents, such as Requests for Proposals or contracts, and from other national studies, including the recently released report from the U.S. Government Accounting Office, *Child Welfare: Early Experiences in Implementing a Managed Care Approach* [1998].

Specifically, the survey asks respondents about:
- the management of child welfare services that are consistent with managed care models—including changes to promote greater efficiency through new gatekeeping or utilization review mechanisms, or the use of single access points where care is coordinated and managed from entry to exit;
- the organization of services—including the creation of provider networks or integrated systems of care, rather than services being delivered by single providers; and
- how services are financed or risk-shared—including risk sharing between purchasers and providers or managed care entities through capped allocations, capitation, case rates, or performance-based contracts.

Forty-nine of the 50 states and the District of Columbia responded (for a response rate of 98%). Of those responding, 29 states reported one or more initiatives that include management or finance changes consistent with managed care or privatization models. This report is an analysis of 47 initiatives in those 29 states.

Results in Brief

Twenty-nine of the 49 states responding to the survey (59%) have one or more initiatives currently underway or planned for implementation within one year. The terms "managed care" or "privatization" were not used by all of the respondents to describe their efforts. Instead, some respondents prefer to report they are using new management tools and funding or contracting strategies to make the system more effective, efficient, and accountable for outcomes.

Public purchasers in most of the current initiatives rely upon private nonprofit agencies to manage and deliver services. However, even when certain public functions are shifted to the private sector, the public agency continues to be an active partner in decisionmaking at key strategic points. For-profit organizations play a significant role in managing services in only three of the 47 initiatives. Nonprofit agencies, on the other hand, are responsible for case management related to permanency planning in 13 initiatives and for case management related to treatment planning, long-term care determination, and placement services in 19 initiatives.

- Seventy-four percent of the initiatives have some financial risk-sharing arrangement in place or planned within the next 12 months. The public purchaser is much more likely to share risks with nonprofit agencies than with for-profit providers. Risk is currently shared with nonprofit agencies in 29 initiatives and with for-profit organizations in two initiatives. In county-administered states, the counties' public agency may also be at financial risk through a capped allocation from the state.

- There is variability in how rates are determined, in the types of risk-sharing arrangements, and in the level of risk borne by contractors. The most common arrangement is a case rate, often including risk adjustment mechanisms to limit losses and profits/savings. In most instances, the risk-adjustment mechanism will protect contractors against catastrophic loss. There have been several notable exceptions where the rate was too low, protection too little, and contractors suffered significant losses.

- Variability in rates proposed for similar initiatives may illustrate how difficult it is to accurately price capitated or case rates in child welfare. For example, case rates for similar populations and services in different states may vary more than $1,200 per child per month.

- As in previous years, there is great variability in the scope of the initiatives. Many states and localities have multiple initiatives underway. All initiatives have different goals, target populations, and services, making comparisons difficult. For example, the largest initiative covers more than 35,000 children, the smallest targets 22 children. Forty-two of the 47 initiatives provided estimates of the number of children to be served annually; the total projected for this year is 114,243. Even though this number is greater than in previous years, it still represents only 10% of the nation's total child welfare population.

- As in previous years, findings indicate that the specific populations vary from one initiative to another with most initiatives targeting children in custody and, specifically, those in out-of-home care settings. But in 1998, there is an increase in the number of initiatives that are also including children at risk of placement. There are also more plans focusing efforts on the families of children in custody and at risk of placement.

- Public agencies report a range of quality assurance mechanisms and reporting requirements to ensure that clients have access to needed care and that contractors are accountable for achieving outcomes consistent with the legal mandates of the system. In the majority of initiatives, the public purchaser has set performance standards related to access, availability, and appropriateness of care and established outcomes related to child and family functioning and permanency. Contractors are being monitored for progress in meeting specified goals. In some instances, financial bonuses and penalties are being linked to performance in key outcome areas.

- There are many different structural designs for the initiatives. In more than half of the initiatives, the public agency is contracting for services in ways that stimulate the development of service delivery networks, often managed by a lead, nonprofit agency, functioning as a managed care entity (MCE). In this report, these are referred to as *lead* agency models. The lead agency assumes varying levels of responsibility for coordinating and providing all the necessary care to the covered population, managing subcontracts with other providers in the network, and delivering some services. In a few initiatives, the MCE is not a provider but rather a managed care organization (MCO) that does not deliver services but is responsible for creating networks and managing the care of all children referred. The lead agency or MCO might operate under a risk-sharing contract or provide services under no-risk contracts.

In other states, the public agency has incorporated managed care practices—such as more rigorous gatekeeping and utilization management procedures or the development of integrated networks of providers—and the public agency functions as the managed care entity. In these initiatives, contracting and payment methods to providers might change but the traditional public/private roles remain intact. In some instances, the public agency has created an interagency collaborative to manage the care of children across systems. In this report, these types of initiatives are referred to as *public agency models*. Public purchasers might also negotiate risk-based contracts with single providers but without the intent to create service networks or relinquish control over most management functions. These are referred to as *single agency models*.

In some initiatives, the public agency contracts for certain administrative services from an *administrative service organization*. These contracts typically involve the management of billing, reimbursement, and client tracking; network training; or MIS development and are usually reimbursed on a no-risk, fee-for-service basis. The ASO (sometimes referred to as a management services organization or MSO) does not have responsibility for providing or coordinating care—this is retained by the public agency or shifted to the lead agency/MCE.

Some initiatives have multiple structural design elements. For example, a public agency might share risks with lead agencies while maintaining fee-for-service arrangements with the ASO. Or, a county agency might have a capped allocation from the state and decide to share risks with single providers. Or, a lead agency might enter into a contract with a managed care organization to provide MIS capability or other administrative services under an ASO contract.

Since the majority of initiatives have been underway less than 12 months, it is too soon to determine long-term results for the children and families served, or to determine which of the various models holds the most promise for child welfare.

CONCLUSIONS

There remains significant diversity among the 47 initiatives, but some similarities and trends are emerging.

When compared with last year's findings, there is an increase in the number of initiatives that are fully underway or in early implementation, rather than still in the planning stage. The increase appears to be due to several factors, including the approval of Title IV-E waivers, which facilitated more flexible use of funds. Legislative mandates also stimulated initiatives in several states.

A few statewide efforts are fully underway, some with expansions into other program areas being planned—including Massachusetts, Kansas, Illinois, and Tennessee. Within the year, Florida will have broadened its privatization pilots to include many more districts. Some initiatives in county-administered states also affect the entire child welfare population. But most plans are still confined to more narrowly defined populations or smaller geographic areas. Nearly all the initiatives include the foster care population and many initiatives are also proposing to cover children at risk of placement and their families. The number of children and families being served under the initiatives is increasing. It is not possible to predict whether the numbers will continue to grow in future years at the same accelerated pace witnessed this past year.

Most initiatives currently use or propose the use of financial risk-sharing arrangements. Due to the uncertainty about accurately pricing child welfare services, many initiatives that include risk-sharing have built in risk adjustment mechanisms to protect against losses that would jeopardize the survival of contractors or the quality of services delivered. The survey cannot determine whether the funds being allocated are sufficient to ensure quality services, improved client outcomes, and system performance over the life of the contract.

Each year the survey is conducted, public respondents seem more knowledgeable about the potential benefits and the risks associated with managed care or privatization. As in past years, public agency administrators do not seem inclined to abandon their missions to for-profit organizations. Instead, they are adapting managed care models to fit the problems in the current system and the unique needs of the population and are limiting the responsibilities delegated to for-profit organizations. The public sector and the nonprofit providers continue to be the dominant forces that are shaping managed care and privatization approaches.

Nearly half of initiatives intend to have an independent evaluation conducted. When evaluations are complete, it will be possible to find out whether these experiments resulted in improved system efficiency and effectiveness, and, most importantly, improved outcomes for children and families. In the short term, most initiatives have placed a premium on the collection of meaningful information about the numbers of children being served, the types of services being delivered, the costs of services, and whether short-term fiscal and programmatic goals are being met. Perhaps one of the greatest benefits of current efforts will be the ability to generate more accurate data about service need characteristics of the populations, utilization patterns and trends over time, and costs that are linked to the attainment of certain outcomes. This alone may improve a system with historically inadequate and inaccurate data on which to base critical decisions.

This report is a conservative estimate of what is going on nationwide. Several states have initiatives underway that were not described in enough detail to be included in this report. Since changes are occurring at a rapid pace, the CWLA Tracking Project database and this report will be updated as new information becomes available.

BACKGROUND & METHODOLOGY

In 1996, prompted by anecdotal evidence that managed care and privatization approaches were being promoted in various state child welfare systems, CWLA's Managed Care Institute (MCI) conducted the first managed care survey of state child welfare administrators in an effort to capture baseline information from all 50 states. That initial survey, a point-in-time descriptive look at managed care, confirmed that many states were interested in learning more about how managed care strategies could be used to make child welfare services more efficient and effective, while containing costs for the most expensive "deep-end" services. This initial survey had limitations, one being a lack of consistency about how respondents were interpreting terms. At that time, it was clear that public administrators were interested in managed care but were not yet familiar or comfortable with some of the basic managed care principles and were not far along in thinking about how managed care could be applied to the child welfare system.

In 1997, using a revised survey instrument as a guide, the MCI developed a tracking project database to allow for the ongoing collection and analysis of managed care/privatization information from all 50 states and selected counties. The database allows the MCI to identify and describe current and potential changes in the way public child welfare agencies are managing, delivering, financing, and contracting for child welfare and related services that are consistent with managed care principles. The database is designed to provide answers to all the questions that must be answered when planning a managed care approach to the management and delivery of child welfare services:

- What are the broad goals of the initiative? What does the public agency hope to accomplish through managed care?
- What population is to be covered by the initiative?
- What services and supports will be included in the plan? What services will be provided outside the plan?
- How will quality be ensured and outcomes defined and measured under the plan?
- How will public and private management roles change under the plan?
- How will the plan be funded and how will risks be shared?

Specifically, the database tracks initiatives that change:

- **the management of child welfare services**—including changes to promote greater efficiency through new gatekeeping or utilization review mechanisms, or the use of single access points where care is coordinated and managed from entry to exit;
- **the organization of services**—including the creation of provider networks or integrated systems of care, rather than services being delivered by single providers; and
- **how services are financed or risk-shared**—including risk sharing between purchasers and providers or managed care entities through capped allocations, capitation, case rates, or performance-based contracts.

In August 1998 the survey instrument was sent to all state child welfare administrators or their designees and to the District of Columbia. State contacts in each of the 12 county-administered states (California, Colorado, Georgia, Maryland, Minnesota, New York, North Carolina, North Dakota, Ohio, Pennsylvania, Virginia, and Wisconsin) were asked to provide an overview of broad state efforts and to recommend a contact from up to five counties who could contribute additional information on any county-specific initiatives.

The survey instrument offered respondents the option to reply by mail or during a telephone interview. During the fall and winter of 1998, telephone interviews were conducted, data were clarified or confirmed, and narrative state profiles were approved by the majority of respondents. The information compiled from the survey served as a foundation for this report. In an attempt to capture the most up-to-date information available, this report also contains information from public documents (i.e., Requests for Proposals, lead agency contracts, and from other national studies, such as the 1998 report from the U.S. Government Accounting Office, *Child Welfare: Early Experiences in Implementing a Managed Care Approach* [GAO 1998]).

The following statistical analysis is based solely on the responses of states and counties that currently have, or are planning to implement within a year, initiatives that apply "managed care" or "privatization" techniques to the management, financing, or delivery of child welfare services. Mental health or behavioral health managed care initiatives that serve child welfare populations were excluded from this report if they did not directly impact the financing, management, or delivery of child welfare services.

The report is limited to initiatives that were described in enough detail to allow for meaningful analysis and contain one or more of the following elements:

- the transfer of primary responsibility for key management functions;
- the introduction of risk-sharing, including the linking of reimbursement to performance standards or outcomes; or
- the creation of provider networks or integrated systems of care.

Some survey respondents took this opportunity to share innovative models for improving child welfare services or management that do not meet the criteria for a "managed care" or privatization initiative. For example, some states have undertaken efforts to install outcomes management systems or develop client and provider profiling capacity. These efforts are not included in the analysis but are summarized in a separate report available through the Managed Care Institute.

Forty-nine of the 50 states and the District of Columbia and 23 of the 36 localities surveyed responded to the survey. This represents a response rate of 98% for the states surveyed and 64% for the localities. Table 1 is a list of states with one or more managed care initiatives.

TABLE 1. STATES AND LOCALITIES WITH ONE OR MORE MANAGED CARE INITIATIVES

State	Initiative
Arizona	Adoption Privatization Initiative; Family Builders
California	Senate Bill 163; San Diego County, Project Heartbeat
Colorado	Capped Allocation to Six Counties, El Paso Protection System; Pikes Peak OPTIONS Behavioral Health Care Network for Foster Care Populations
Connecticut	Continuum of Care: Title IV-E waiver
Delaware	CPS Low-Risk Intervention
Florida	Statewide Privatization Initiative; Pilots in Districts 4, 1, 8, and 13
Georgia	MATCH (Multi-Agency Team for Children)
Hawaii	Ohana Family Conferencing
Illinois	Performance Contracting
Indiana	Child Welfare Waiver Demonstration
Kansas	Privatization Initiatives for Foster Care; Adoption; and Family Preservation
Kentucky	Quality Care Pilot
Maryland	Baltimore City
Massachusetts	Commonworks; Family-Based Initiatives
Michigan	Michigan Families Title IV-E Waiver; Adoption Contracting; Permanency-Focused Reimbursement System Pilot
Minnesota	Hennepin County Children's Mental Health Collaborative
Missouri	Interdepartmental Children's Service Initiative
New York	New York City ACS Community Assistance Reinvestment; Neighborhood-Based Initiative in the Bronx
North Carolina	Title IV-E Waiver Capped Allocation to 19 Counties; Buncombe County
Ohio	Title IV-E Waiver for 14 Counties; Crawford, Cuyahoga, Franklin, Hamilton, and Lorain Counties
Oklahoma	Children's Services Initiative
Pennsylvania	Berk County
South Carolina	Privatized Adoption Services
Tennessee	Nonresidential Networks; Continuum of Care Contracts
Texas	Project PACE (Permanency Achieved Through Coordinated Efforts)
Utah	Residential Contract Restructuring
Washington	Capitated Payment for Children with Special Needs; Title IV-E Waiver
West Virginia	Region IV Foster Care Pilot
Wisconsin	Case Management Contracts

PRINCIPAL FINDINGS

Twenty-nine states have one or more initiatives that change management, contracting, financing, or service delivery practices using managed care tools or principles or privatization approaches (see Table 2). This represents 59% of the 49 states that responded to the survey. A total of 47 initiatives are analyzed in this report and described in the attached state profiles.

Note: Some states and counties reported on multiple initiatives, providing more than one response to each question. Therefore, throughout this document, the numbers given for any question may not equal the number of states or counties reporting, but rather the number of initiatives.

SIMILARITIES AND DIFFERENCES IN GOALS, SCOPE, AND DESIGN OF INITIATIVES

There is significant diversity among initiatives in scope and design. There are also similarities in the broad goals of the initiatives.

Broad Goals

Most managed care plans appear to be conceived as a way to improve the current child welfare system, and there is some consistency among the initiatives in the stated goals. Each survey respondent was asked to identify the four most important goals for the initiative. The seven most frequently cited goals are listed below:

TABLE 2. NUMBER OF INITIATIVES REPORTING MANAGED CARE OR PRIVATIZATION APPROACHES TO THE MANAGEMENT, FINANCE, OR DELIVERY OF CHILD WELFARE SERVICES (N=47)

	Currently Implementing Changes	Implementing Changes Within 1 Year	Not Part of the Initiative
Management Changes	32	13	2
Service Delivery Changes	27	12	8
Financing or Contract Changes	26	18	3

- Improve client outcomes,
- Achieve permanency in the shortest time,
- Decrease length of stay in out-of-home care,
- Improve the quality of services,
- Create a more seamless system,
- Maintain children in their own homes and communities, and
- Provide individualized and accessible care.

Scope and Timetable for Implementation

There is great variability in the scope of initiatives and timetables for implementing managed care or privatization efforts. A few states have already implemented statewide or large countywide initiatives, affecting entire child welfare populations and broad service areas. For example, the Kansas Family Preservation, Foster Care, and Adoption initiatives privatized the management and service delivery of all child welfare services (with the exception of CPS intake and investigation) through case rate contracts across the state with lead agencies (nonprofit providers) that function as managed care entities. The state's privatization contracts total $102 million and account for 56% of child welfare spending in Kansas.

In other states the percent of spending for initiatives varies from less than 2% to nearly one-third of the budget. For example, in Illinois, in FY99, the budget for the Performance Contracting initiative is $334 million, representing approximately one-fourth of the state child welfare budget. The Commonworks program, a statewide initiative in Massachusetts that serves approximately 1000 children in need of group or residential care, has a budget of approximately $45 million for FY99, or about 11% of the state's total child welfare budget. Ohio is in the process of implementing its Title IV-E waiver demonstration in 14 of its 88 counties. Funding for ProtectOhio for FY 99 is $49 million, or about 9% of the state's child welfare budget. However, since the county initiatives in Ohio varied greatly in size and scope, the percent varies from one county to another. In Franklin County, OH the waiver demonstration accounts for 15% of the total county child welfare budget. Hamilton County, OH has two initiatives that combine to account for more than 30% of the county's total child welfare spending.

Most states are moving slowly, using pilot programs to test various changes before developing a statewide plan. In 1997, Florida began its entry into privatization with relatively small pilots in four geographic regions of the state. The state now has a legislative mandate to privatize foster care and all related services statewide over the course of the next few years, using lead agency contracts that will shift significant financial risk to contractors. In Colorado, under a legislative mandate, the state agency, after an RFP process, selected three pilot counties (Mesa, Jefferson, and Boulder Counties) to test out new ways of managing services under a capped allocation from the state in 1997. About that same time, a fourth county, El Paso, was also allowed to begin to implement several managed care initiatives. Performance in the pilot counties has been promising and, under legislative change in 1998, the state added additional counties for full implementation this year.

Even when states intend to launch a statewide, comprehensive managed care or privatized model, they may start with one service area or covered population and gradually expand the initiative. For example, Arizona hopes to get legislative support to change how services are managed and delivered for the entire child welfare system, but the state proposes to start with adoption services, then phase in family preservation and foster care services over time.

Size of the Initiatives and Covered Populations

The survey attempted to find out which of the children and families in a community or state would be covered by the proposed initiative. Would plans cover all children who are at risk of abuse or neglect? Only those who come to the attention of child welfare after an allegation of abuse or neglect? Only those children with substantiated abuse or neglect histories? Only those children in need of out-of-home care placement? Only those children in the most restrictive, intensive out-of-home care settings? Or, only those children in out-of-home care with Serious Emotional Disturbance diagnoses? Would initiatives cover the families of these children? If so, what services and supports would be provided to them?

As in previous years, findings indicate that the specific populations vary from one initiative to another with most initiatives targeting children in out-of-home care settings. But in 1998, there is an increase in the number of initiatives that are also including children at risk of placement and there are also more plans focusing efforts on the families of children in custody and at risk of placement. In most instances, however, initiatives that propose to cover broad populations will initially cover only those children and families in certain demonstration or pilot regions, or a sample of children that is limited to a predetermined number.

The initiatives vary in size from less than 25 to more than 35,000 children and families served. Forty-two initiatives reported on the projected number of children to be served this year; the total was 114,243. Table 3 summarizes the size range of the 42 initiatives which reported that information.

Services and Supports

A central tenet of an effective managed care system is that a full array of services are in place to ensure that individuals can access the services they need, when they need them, in the appropriate amount and intensity, to achieve desired outcomes in the most cost-effective manner. The survey instrument was designed to determine which services are included in each of the initiatives.

Service areas covered by the various current or proposed initiatives vary, as they did in 1997, but most of the initiatives include out-of-home care options above the level of traditional family foster care. Child Protective Service (CPS) intake and investigations and postadoption supports and services are least likely to be included. Case management is the most likely service to be included. Continuing a trend identified in 1997, it appears that some initiatives are focusing attention on the front-end of the child welfare system and are including a variety of services to prevent placement for at-risk families before or after the investigation phase of CPS. For example, Arizona's Family Builders provides family support and preservation services through collaborative community networks in which low-risk CPS cases are managed by lead agencies under case rates. Delaware's

Table 3. Size of the Initiatives (N=42)

Annual Number of Children Served	Number and Percent of Initiatives Implementing or Planning Changes at This Time
Serving less than 100 children	4 (10%)
Serving between 100-299 children	9 (21%)
Serving between 300-499 children	5 (12%)
Serving between 500-999 children	6 (14%)
Serving between 1,000-1,999 children	5 (12%)
Serving 2,000 or more children	13 (31%)

Low Risk Intervention targets families that have been investigated by CPS and identified as low risk for a range of therapeutic and family support services.

This year's survey also indicates that an increasing number of initiatives are including services to the families of children in custody and families of children at risk of entering custody. For example, there is an increase in the number of initiatives that report the inclusion of "wraparound" approaches to reduce the need for initial placement, to shorten the length of stay in placement, and to prevent reentry into placement for children who have returned home.

Table 4 lists the services most likely to be included under an initiative.

Structural Design of the Initiatives

As in previous years, there are many different structural designs for the initiatives. There does now appear to be a trend towards creating provider networks, however. In more than half of the initiatives, the public agency is contracting for services in ways that stimulate the development of service delivery networks, managed by a lead, nonprofit agency, functioning as a managed care entity. In this report, these are referred to as *lead agency models*.

In some localities, provider agencies created alliances or formed new managed care entities prior to the release of an RFP. This was the case in Missouri where the Missouri Alliance, a limited liability corporation, was formed by nonprofit agencies a year before the state released an interdepartmental RFP. The Missouri Alliance was recently awarded the three-year lead agency contract to manage the care of up to 1,500 of the state's children with severe needs beginning in February 1999. In other localities, the RFP required the submission of collaborative proposals, encouraging

Table 4. Services Included in the Initiatives

Services Included in the Initiatives	Percentage of Initiatives
Case management	79%
Mental health services	66%
Treatment foster care	66%
Wraparound services	62%
Family preservation and support services	60%
Group care	57%
Respite care	57%
Family foster care	55%
Residential treatment	55%
Permanency planning	53%
Independent living	51%

potential bidders to organize themselves prior to being awarded the contract. In most instances, the development of a network was an explicit RFP requirement for lead agencies, but the network was not created until after the lead agency contract was awarded.

The lead agency assumes varying levels of responsibility for coordinating and providing all the necessary care to the covered population, managing subcontracts with other providers in the network, and delivering some services. In some initiatives, lead agencies operate under no-risk contracts but in many initiatives they now operate under case rates. The Massachusetts Commonworks initiative is the oldest lead agency initiative in the country. The state agency initially contracted with six lead agencies, covering different regions of the state, under a no-risk arrangement. After accurate data were available to determine utilization and true costs, lead agencies began operating under a case rate in the summer of 1998. Some initiatives that use a lead agency model place limits on the amount of direct services lead agencies are allowed to provide. For example, in Massachusetts, the lead agency may not provide more than 25% of the services directly. In a few initiatives, the MCE is not a provider but rather a managed care organization (MCO) that is responsible for creating networks and managing the care of all children referred.

In other states, the public agency has incorporated managed care practices—such as more rigorous gatekeeping and utilization management procedures or the creation of cross-system public collaboratives—and the public agency functions as the managed care entity. In these initiatives, contracting and payment methods to providers might change but the traditional public/private roles remain intact. In some instances, public agencies across systems have created an interagency collaborative to manage the care of children. The collaborative might also have a designated lead public agency that bears risk for managing care and resources within a set budget. The Michigan IV-E demonstration, Michigan's Families, is one example of this model. The state agency issued an RFP for the development of collaborative proposals from up to six different regions of the state to develop wraparound approaches for children in care or at risk of placement. The collaborative was required to have participation of certain public agencies, including the community mental health agencies, and each collaborative had to name a lead fiduciary agency that would bear financial risk. (In Michigan, all Medicaid behavioral health dollars are administered by the community mental health boards.) The collaborative will receive a monthly case rate of $1,500 for Title IV-E eligible children to cover the costs of wraparound and other services. But, each collaborative agency will also contribute funding to support services outside the case rate. In this report, these types of initiatives are referred to as *public agency models*. Public models do not require public agencies or providers to change traditional roles and therefore may be easier for public agencies to design and manage.

Public purchasers are also negotiating risk-based contracts with single providers but without the requirement that they create or manage service networks or assume control over most management functions. These are referred to as *single agency models*. Under this model, the public agency may retain responsibility for many key decisions while incentivizing providers to achieve desired programmatic outcomes. In Michigan, for example, the state agency manages permanency and adoption performance-based contracts that share risks with single providers, with the public agency retaining many traditional management responsibilities.

In some initiatives, the public agency or a lead agency contracts for certain administrative services from an *administrative service organization*. These contracts typically involve the management of billing, reimbursement, client tracking, network training, or MIS development and are reimbursed on a fee-for-service basis, not involving financial risk. The ASO (sometimes referred to as a management services organization or MSO) does not have responsibility for providing or coordinating care—this is retained by the public agency or shifted to the lead agency/MCE. For example, both Massachusetts and Missouri use an ASO in addition to their lead agency. In both states, the contract was awarded to ValueOptions. The reimbursement to the ASO is approximately 5% of the total budget for the initiatives in both states.

Many initiatives, such as Massachusetts and Missouri, have multiple structural design elements. For example, a public agency shares risks with lead agencies while maintaining fee for service arrangements with the ASO. Or, a county agency has a capped allocation from the state and decides to share risks and decisionmaking responsibility with single providers. In addition, a lead agency might enter into a contract with a managed care organization to provide MIS capability or other administrative services under an ASO contract. Less frequently, traditional nonprofit providers in partnership with a national behavioral health organization create a new managed care entity to share risks and management responsibilities. While there is a trend toward the use of nonprofit lead agencies, it is likely that many other variations on the theme will continue to surface.

QUALITY AND OUTCOMES ACCOUNTABILITY

The twin promises of managed care—cost containment and access to quality care—have to be closely monitored. The use of managed care tools will not guarantee nor preclude an efficient system of quality services for children and families. Conscious effort is needed to ensure that managed care or privatization initiatives include specific quality indicators to assess both system performance and client specific outcomes. The survey assesses whether the initiatives include system performance indicators that relate to access to services, appropriateness of services, quality of providers, cultural competency, client satisfaction, and fiscal performance. In addition to these important elements, the legal mandates of child welfare related to safety and permanency should provide the context for any child welfare plan. So, the survey asks about client outcomes related to permanency and child and family well-being and functioning.

Most current or proposed child welfare managed care or privatized initiatives define outcomes and indicators that are consistent with the mandates and core values of child welfare, but plans do differ in the central focus and in the ways that performance will be measured and evaluated. For example, some states are most interested in reducing length of stay or level of care for children already in the foster care system; other initiatives are primarily intended to prevent initial entry or make better initial assessments to match children to the most appropriate services and levels of care through an improved utilization management system.

Purchasers have been most likely to include performance indicators related to effectiveness of services (78%) in their RFPs or contracts. Achievement of the permanency plan goals is a specified outcome in 31 initiatives (67%). It is interesting that 67% of the initiatives have a customer satisfaction requirement. In some cases satisfaction data will be collected through surveys at the conclusion of services by an outside party. In other initiatives, focus groups and ongoing assessment of satisfaction are required. Many initiatives track and report on the active involvement of families in addition to traditional consumer satisfaction surveys. Twenty-one (46%) of the initiatives will have an independent evaluation—a requirement for all Title IV-E demonstration sites. (The MCI has developed a white paper that examines outcomes in child welfare managed care plans in greater detail.) Table 5 shows the number of initiatives that reported that they are incorporating quality requirements or outcome measures related to each of the following areas.

States and counties are using multiple means to collect and manage quality and outcomes data. Since managed care systems are information-driven, many of the plans rely heavily on reports generated from the automated MIS and provided to the state by the lead agency, managed care entity, or individual service providers. Table 6 describes the sources of outcomes and quality information for the initiatives.

Almost all of the initiatives report that they are holding providers accountable for achieving certain performance standards or improving outcomes for children and families. That is most encouraging. As yet, however, it is not clear in the vast majority of initiatives whether improvements have resulted. The efforts to document the results of an initiative have been hampered by the lack of baseline data. Most initiatives have had to collect baseline data and then track performance over time to document success.

The results of internal evaluations of some state and county initiatives show promise—Illinois; El Paso County, Colorado; and the Florida pilots, for example. Performance contracting was initially implemented in Cook County, Illinois for relative foster care in July 1997. During the first year, the relative foster care caseload declined for the first time in over a

Table 5. Quality Requirements and Outcomes Measures

Quality Requirements and Outcome Measures	Number & Percent of Initiatives Incorporating
Performance indicators related to effectiveness	36 (78%)
Achievement of permanency planning goals	31 (67%)
Consumer satisfaction requirement	31 (67%)
Outcomes related to child functioning	29 (63%)
Specific criteria related to cost	29 (63%)
Outcomes related to family functioning	28 (61%)
Outcomes related to recidivism/reentry	27 (59%)
Access/availability/utilization standards	26 (57%)
Requirements to adhere to professional standards or licensing requirements	24 (52%)
Credentialing requirements for individual providers	24 (52%)
Specific cultural competence criteria or standards	23 (50%)
Independent evaluation of the initiative	21 (46%)
Specific criteria related to appropriateness of services	21 (46%)
Level of care criteria or clinical protocols	13 (28%)
National accreditation of agencies/facilities	12 (26%)

Table 6. Methods Used to Gather Outcome and Quality Information

Sources of Information	Percentage of Initiatives Utilizing
Utilization, cost, and performance data from MIS tracking	72%
Reports from providers	67%
Reports from families	50%
Standardized assessments	50%
Reports from schools	28%
Pre- and post-tests	28%

decade—decreasing 15%. Performance contracting also helped boost the adoption and guardianship rates in Cook County home of relative care from 0.5 per 100 child cases during the third quarter of FY97 to 6.2 per 100 child cases during the first quarter of FY98. In addition, instability rates were cut in half and an estimated 250 children remained in less restrictive and less costly placements. Current data suggest to the Illinois Department that the promising trends are sustainable. As of December 1998, the Cook County relative care caseload was at 18,892. The state anticipates the July 1999 contracted caseload in Cook County relative care to be approximately 16,715. This represents a decline of 7,726 cases or 32% over a two-year period.

But, results have been mixed in other sites. It is possible that initiatives may meet or exceed performance in some key quality areas, but fail to meet expectations in others. This has been the experience in the Kansas Foster Care Privatization contracts. Lead agencies have met or exceeded expectations of the state on some performance indicators but have been less successful in other areas. For example, the lead agencies have not met the target timelines for achieving permanency through reunification. The state acknowledges that the initial targets were not based on any accurate baseline data and may have been unrealistically high.

States that had hoped for dramatic cost savings have probably been disappointed. In most instances the best that could be expected with available funding was cost neutrality but with improved quality and access to services by greater numbers of children and families in need.

Management Changes and Financial Risk-Sharing

A major change associated with managed care is the introduction of shared financial risk and shared authority for critical decisionmaking between contractors that bear risk and public agencies. Since there are so many possible options for sharing management tasks in child welfare, it is not surprising that the 1998 survey reveals significant variations among the initiatives. The risk-sharing arrangement and the responsibility for various management functions may even vary within the same initiative over time, or from one county initiative to another within the same state.

Many initiatives link financial bonuses and penalties to the performance indicators in the contract with single providers, lead agencies, ASOs, or other public or private entities. Sometimes the linkage is implied and at other times, the contract is quite explicit. For example, some contracts provide a lump sum bonus at the end of a set time for any child that remains safely in a permanent placement. Less explicit but obvious are the provisions that allow agencies operating under a case rate to retain a certain percent of savings. They will benefit if they are successful in achieving permanency in a shorter than projected time. In the contract between the Hamilton County Ohio Department of Human Services and Magellan Public Solutions, Magellan can earn as much as $100,000 per year in bonuses for meeting certain system performance standards. It can earn additional bonuses if the county saves more money than was projected, but Magellan could also lose up to $65,000 for failing to meet certain quality indicators.

In some states or counties, the public agency retains responsibility for most decisions but contracts with providers in ways that link reimbursement to the attainment of certain outcomes—thereby sharing limited risks. In other instances, the public agency contracts for certain administrative functions with a managed care entity (a for-profit MCE, a nonprofit single provider, or lead agency) but retains responsibility for critical case management decisions. In still other instances, the public agency contracts with a MCE (a for-profit managed care organization, nonprofit lead agency, or an entity that is created from a joint venture between for-profit and nonprofit organizations) to develop and manage a provider network and make virtually all care management decisions. In county-administered states, the state agency may share risks with county agencies under new capped allocations. Under such arrangements, it is likely the county agency is also given increased responsibility for managing resources and risks and retaining savings. The county agency may then decide to share risks and management responsibilities with providers or lead agencies.

It is difficult to assess through a survey whether the level of risk being assumed by a contractor is always accompanied by increased control over management decisions and how limited resources are used.

Public and Private Agency Decisionmaking: Changing Roles

There are many ways the responsibility for managing child welfare services can be divided between public and private agencies. Even when services are managed and delivered by private agencies that are bearing financial risks, however, public agencies tend to remain involved to varying degrees in decisionmaking at key strategic points. In all instances, as in previous years' findings, the survey reveals that the public agency has retained primary responsibility for CPS intake and investigations and for determining which children require protective services or custody. If a managed care or privatized initiative is in place, the referral to the plan is done or approved by the public agency. In that regard the public agency remains the child welfare system's gatekeeper.

In many other instances where public agencies are sharing responsibility with contractors for ongoing case management and even permanency planning, contractors are still required to get prior approval before making certain decisions. For example, in the majority of initiatives, private contractors could not change a permanency plan for a child without approval of the public agency or the court. Private contractors might be able to manage treatment services and make clinical determinations without approval of the public agency, but they would not usually be allowed to disenroll a child or terminate services without approval. When level of care determinations are made or service plans changed or developed, the public agency requires notification, if not prior approval.

Even when public agencies contract with a lead agency for the creation and management of a provider network, the public agency may exercise some control over the subcontracting process. For example, the network that was created by Magellan Public Solutions in Hamilton County, Ohio, was initially selected by the county agency through an RFP process. Many initiatives that allow lead agencies or managed care entities to subcontract with providers include stipulations that the public agency must approve all subcontractors and reimbursement rates.

All of this being said, it is clear that many private, nonprofit agencies under contract with public purchasers are assuming many responsibilities formerly held by public agencies. In fact, many managed care contracts make it clear that the public purchaser views the contractor as a partner to be entrusted with the care management of even the most difficult to serve children and youth. It is also clear in many initiatives that this responsibility should not be taken lightly by contractors. To underscore this point, many initiatives include no eject/no reject language. The contractor may not refuse a child who meets the referral criteria and, once accepted, the child may not be ejected from the program or network.

Many nonprofit providers have also taken on unfamiliar administrative tasks and had to learn about federal and state claiming and reimbursement systems. All contractors bearing financial risks have had to develop new risk management skills. Since all contracts require some quality and outcomes reporting, nonprofit agencies have had to develop mechanisms for documenting utilization and the results of services in new ways. In the case of lead agencies, they have had to develop contract management and monitoring skills and learn how to manage and coordinate the care of individual children outside their agency walls. And, last but not least, one expectation public agencies have for contractors is that they will be able to generate and manage timely, accurate information on the characteristics of children and families served, the services provided, and the costs of care. Private contractors have had to acquire or enhance their MIS capability to meet these strict reporting requirements.

The survey attempts to find out whether certain management tools or practices, consistent with managed care systems, are included in the initiatives. The survey asked respondents about responsibility for various functions, including the following:

- pre-authorization for care;
- gatekeeping;
- utilization management, including both prospective, concurrent, and retrospective review;
- creation of provider networks and contract management with providers;
- tracking of data related to outcomes, expenditures, quality, etc;
- case management related to permanency planning;
- case management related to treatment decisions;
- billing, reimbursement, claims adjudication; and
- handling grievance and appeals.

Respondents were also asked to identify the entity—the public state or county child welfare agency, a for-profit MCE, a nonprofit provider or lead agency, or other public agency (Medicaid or Mental Health Authority, for example)—responsible for each function.

The survey results indicate great diversity in how current and proposed initiatives will handle various management functions. In general, public agencies retain responsibility for Medicaid and Title IV-E eligibility determination, contracting with MCEs, overseeing and approving the development of certain level of care or service necessity criteria, monitoring performance in key outcome and quality areas, and ensuring payment for services. It is most common for public agencies to contract for provider network development, provider subcontract management, utilization management, reimbursement to providers in the network, quality monitoring, tracking of outcomes, and other critical data-reporting functions. Contracts for these functions could be with managed care entities that could be either a nonprofit "lead" agency or a for-profit MCO.

Since management functions are shared by public agency and contractor staff, many initiatives include some innovative staffing arrangements.

For example, in one Florida pilot, public agency staff members are assigned to the contractor's multidisciplinary team.

There is evidence that provider networks are becoming more common as a means of ensuring a more seamless system of care. The contractor responsible for this function might be a MCO that does not deliver services or it might be a lead agency that both manages the network and continues to provide services directly. In 49% of the initiatives, private agencies are responsible for creating networks; in 26% of the initiatives this is the responsibility of the public agency. Ten (21%) of the initiatives do not include the creation of networks.

Different Financial Risk-Sharing Arrangements

Seventy-four percent of the initiatives currently include or plan to include financial incentives or financial risk. Like all other areas of the survey, states vary in their approaches to risk—both in terms of the nature of the risk and how risk will be introduced into initiatives. When risk-sharing has been introduced, it has typically been between the public agency and a nonprofit entity.

The level of risk ranges from capped allocations or capitation to case rates to lower risk performance-based, incentivized contracts. In the purest managed care model, a contractor is prepaid on a monthly basis, a fixed amount for all contracted services for a defined, enrolled client population. This per-member, per-month population-based payment arrangement is referred to as *capitation*. Under this arrangement, the contractor receives the predetermined monthly amount, based on enrollment, regardless of the level of services that enrolled clients require during the month. If the contractor succeeds in enrolling clients who then underutilize services, the contractor makes money. On the other hand, the contractor is exposed to significant financial risks if the plan is not priced right, or if the eligible, enrolled population requires more services or more costly services than projected. As an example, El Paso County, Colorado has a capitated contract with Pikes Peak OPTIONS, a managed behavioral health organization, to manage all of the behavioral health services needed by all children enrolled in the plan.

Capitation rates must be based on accurate projections of the service needs of the general population in the geographic region covered by the plan. Since no one can project with any degree of certainty the numbers of children and families within a given community who might enter the child welfare system, it has been difficult if not impossible to accurately price a child welfare capitation model that is based on the general population. And, even if the number of possible enrollees is known, no one can yet project the types, intensity, and duration of services needed once a child and family enter the system, making pricing even more challenging. For these and many other reasons, pure capitation is not a common model for sharing risks in child welfare.

State agencies, however, find the predictability in costs under capitation reimbursement quite attractive. There are several initiatives that include reimbursement methods which resemble capitation in that they include a predetermined payment to cover all services needed for the targeted population. For example, in many of the county-administered initiatives the state provides the county a capped allocation and the county assumes responsibility for managing and delivering child welfare services under this "block grant." In addition to county initiatives, nonprofit Florida agencies in Sarasota and Lake and Sumter Counties operate under what is often referred to as capitated contracts. They are given a predetermined percent of the state's annual operating budget and asked to provide all services, in whatever amount needed, regardless of how many children and families in their geographic area need care. (The allocation is based in part on historic caseload size for the geographic area covered.) This method is also sometimes called a *global budget*.

A more common risk-sharing model in child welfare managed care initiatives is a *case rate*. Under this arrangement, a provider, lead agency, or other managed care entity is paid a predetermined amount for each client referred. In child welfare contracts, the case rate could be episodic or annual. An episodic rate means the contractor must provide all the services from initial entry into the plan until the episode ends. The point at which risk ends varies from one initiative to another. However, it is common for the contractor to bear some risk until specified goals are met, whether that takes days, weeks, or years. For example, a typical case rate contract for foster care services extends financial risks for up to 12 months after the child leaves the foster care system. If the child reenters care during that time, the contractor may bear some or all costs for placement services. The contract for adoption services in Kansas holds lead agencies at risk for 18 months after the adoption is finalized.

Public agencies have less predictability under case rates than capitation and if utilization goes up, the public agency may prefer to negotiate a capitated arrangement. This was the case in the Bridges Program in Lake and Sumter Counties, Florida. Initially the contract agency examined the actual costs of caring for children in out-of-home care and in their own homes, looking back over a two-year period. The agency bundled administrative and direct care costs into a two-year case rate of approximately $15,000 for each child referred. (This rate is based on a daily cost of $21 per child per day.) The contract agency was able to use the case rate to provide both in-home and out-of-home care services and sometimes successfully closed cases before the end of the two years, while continuing to receive reimbursement. However, the state abandoned the case rate because it could not claim federal Title IV-E reimbursement for children who were no longer in the foster care system and the state was having to pay the per diem with state funds. The contractor now operates under a capped allocation for the entire caseload and not a rate for individual cases.

The other form of risk sharing found in initiatives is performance-based contracting. It is usually less risky for providers than either capitation or case rates and is easier for public agencies to design. The goal is to incentivize providers to achieve the outcomes desired by the purchaser. Under performance-based contracts, public purchasers link reimbursement rates or payment schedules to the achievement of specified performance indicators or client outcomes. These incentivized contracts might include either bonuses or penalties or a combination of both. For example, the Illinois Performance Contracts for foster care and kinship care contain both bonuses and penalties and providers have the opportunity to benefit or lose in several ways:

- Agencies that move more than the contracted number of children into permanent living arrangements do not experience a reduction in case management payments.

- Agencies that move more than the contracted number of children into permanent living arrangements may receive up to $2,000 per permanency outcome above the standard payment. Each placement that results in a "pay-out" will be replaced with another referral.

- An agency could lose up to 33% of its contract in one year if it does not achieve the performance standards included in the contract because it will not continue to receive referrals.

- An agency's contract may be cancelled if its uncompensated care (cases in excess of the payment level) exceeds 20% of its total caseload.

Purchasers could also discount the normal fee-for-service payment and withhold a portion until certain outcomes are achieved. This is the model used in Wisconsin's Case Management Initiative in Milwaukee County. For the first year the lead agency was reimbursed for 95% of the actual allowable costs reported on each month's expenditure report. The lead agency received an additional 5% if the following requirements were met:

- For 90% of all new cases assigned, the Family Assessments and Treatment Plans are completed within 60 days of the assignment; and
- For 90% of the Treatment Plans, the Case Evaluation is completed every 90 days.

The lead agencies are also eligible to receive additional payment based on the ability to reduce costs of out-of-home care. If the actual costs during the second year fall short of what has been projected, the department intends to distribute a portion of the savings to the lead agencies. Those agencies achieving the greatest savings will receive the greatest return.

It is also possible to design a contract with case rates that include bonuses or penalties. For example, in addition to the amount of the case rate, lead agencies could be given "lump sum" bonuses that are attached to overall fiscal or programmatic performance. The Connecticut Continuum of Care contract will reward lead agencies up to 10% of the final case rate for the successful and timely completion of the treatment plan, and Delaware's Low Risk initiative will reward lead agencies $250 for each successful case closure within six months with no re-report within one year.

The schedule for reimbursement can also be linked to performance. For example, in the new South Carolina Adoption contracts, agencies are paid when they achieve certain milestones. The maximum case rate payable under this contract is $13,000 per child or $15,700 per sibling group. But the state reimburses contractors based on the following schedule:

- The contractor receives $3,000 at the time a child or sibling group is placed in an adoptive or pre-adoptive home;
- The contractor is paid $375 for each month, up to a maximum of $4,500 for up to 12 months after the placement, during the time the contractor is supervising the placement. In the case of a sibling group, the monthly payment is $600 up to a maximum of $7,200;
- The department pays any board payments or adoption subsidies or benefits directly to the family;

- The contractor is paid $4,000 when the final adoption decree is received; and
- The contractor is paid the remaining $1,500 six months after the final decree if the adoptive placement is still intact.

In the Michigan Permanency Focused Initiative, contractors are paid an initial lump-sum payment of approximately $1,770 for each eligible youth referred. Contractors receive an additional $14.94 per day for each child referred. An additional lump sum payment of $1,500 is made for each eligible youth if either of the following are true: parental rights have been terminated within 600 days (Wayne County) or 420 days (outstate) from the acceptance date; or a successful placement had been made within 315 days (Wayne County) or 265 days (outstate) from the acceptance date. Finally, a provider receives a single lump-sum payment of $730 for each youth who sustains a successful placement for at least six consecutive months, or is placed for adoption within six months of termination of parental rights. Youth who return to the foster care system within one year from the date of a "successful placement" are not eligible for a delayed payment, but are eligible for an initial payment and the per diem rate.

Risk Adjustment Mechanisms

Many contracts that call for risk-sharing are including some risk-adjusted mechanisms to ensure that contractors remain solvent and stable. Because of the uncertainty in calculating reimbursement rates, different methods are used to limit a contractor's risk. Of the agencies that currently share financial risk (31) or intend to share risk within the year (7), 32% (12) will include some risk adjustment mechanism and 40% (15) have not yet determined whether they will use a risk adjustment mechanism.

There are many ways public purchasers can limit contractor risks. In some initiatives, the public agency will contract for certain services under fee-for-service arrangements outside the fixed rate. For example, many child welfare case rates cover certain services typically reimbursed under IV-E funds, but the contractor is expected to bill Medicaid for other services reimbursed under fee-for-service arrangements. In the Texas PACE initiative, the lead agency, Lena Pope Home, Inc., will receive $72.40 per-child per-day to cover out-of-home care placement and maintenance costs, regardless of the level of care (LOC) of the child. This represents an average of the full LOC rates for contracted 24-hour out-of-home care in the Dallas-

Fort Worth region. Lena Pope Home, Inc. and providers in the network will be need to use Medicaid funds to the greatest extent possible to supplement the case rate to support the therapeutic services and assessment services they provide.

In other instances, the contract includes either aggregate or individual stop-loss provisions that limit the contractor's losses when expenditures exceed a certain amount for either an individual case or for the entire covered population. The contract specifies how excess costs are shared between the contractor and the public purchaser. In a few initiatives the contractor is allowed to select a certain number of cases to be reimbursed outside the risk arrangement on a fee for service basis. For example, following the completion of the first year of the Kansas foster care privatization initiative it was apparent that the risk-sharing corridor, as defined in the initial contract, was inadequate for the needs of the lead foster care agencies. During contract renewal, the state made the following case rate adjustments: the foster care case rate was increased by $1,500 per case for all year two referrals, and each lead agency was allowed to assign 150 children per year to traditional fee-for-service reimbursement.

Another method used to limit risk is to require a risk pool to cover the unexpected high costs for certain individuals or groups of children. Both the public agency and the contractor might contribute to the risk pool and the terms for its use would be described in the contract. To protect against uncertainty about the size of the population, the purchaser can also guarantee the contractor a minimum and maximum number of referrals.

In addition to protecting contractors from excessive loss, ten initiatives also limit the contractor's ability to retain profits or savings. The ceiling for loss will probably be the same for retained profits. If the contractor cannot lose more than 5%, it is likely they cannot retain more than 5% in savings. Contracts specify how savings above a certain percent are to be reinvested into the system.

The Introduction of Risk into the Initiative: How Does the Price Get Set?

Some initiatives will introduce financial risk-sharing from the initial implementation. Others will phase in risk after some period of time—often after the first year of cost and utilization data collection and analysis.

The reimbursement rate is set in various ways. In some initiatives, the public agency provided a spending ceiling in the Request for Proposal and allowed the competitive bidding process to set the price parameters that were then negotiated in final contracts. The challenge with this method is that providers who are eager to win the business but inexperienced in managing risk-based contracts may seriously underprice their services.

The public agency can also put a price on the services when the RFP is released. Bidders may then have to determine if they can survive the rate being proposed. This was the method used by the Missouri Interdepartmental Children's Services Initiative. If the public agency sets the rate, it is likely that the agency began by examining historical costs of purchasing similar services. It is also likely that the rate will not include the full costs of delivering and managing services or any provisions for start-up costs. Under most initiatives, regardless of how the rate is determined, it appears that the public agency expects the contractor to supplement the contract rate with funds from other sources—either other state or local dollars, grants or charitable dollars, or federal programs such as Medicaid. This expectation is explicit in most RFPs and contracts.

The rates being proposed are difficult to compare from one initiative to another, since the scope of the initiatives and the populations covered vary greatly. However, it does appear that there is significant variability in rates even among relatively similar plans. For example, both the Commonworks initiative in Massachusetts and the Interdepartmental Children's Services Initiative in Missouri provide "deep-end" services for children with SED needs. Both states use a lead agency model with an ASO contract for administrative support services. The Massachusetts' lead agencies operated without risk initially until costs and utilization data could be used to negotiate rates. Lead agencies are now paid a per-child, per-month case rate of $4,447 to provide any and all services covered under the initiative until the case is closed. In Missouri the lead agency will assume risk when the program begins operation in February 1999. The RFP specified that the lead agency will receive a per-child, per-month rate of approximately $3,200 to provide all needed services.

Funding Sources

The needs of the children and families served by child welfare cut across multiple systems and agencies. To deliver coordinated, integrated services to both children and families, funds need to be maximized at the federal level across several programs and pooled, shared, or blended at the local or state level. While the majority of initiatives still rely heavily or entirely upon child welfare funds, there is some indication in the survey that agencies are increasingly combining funds from multiple federal, state, or local funding sources to support their initiatives.

What is less clear in the survey is whether the amount of funds allocated for an initiative are sufficient to meet the specified goals. In most state or county initiatives, there is an expectation that the initiative(s) will result in improved services and better outcomes for children. It appears, however, that the level of projected funding from the various federal, state, and local sources, does not increase over prior spending. Over the upcoming year, the Tracking Project will try to better assess how federal, state, and local funds from different sources, are being used to support the initiatives and to try to calculate the average spending per child/family across all the initiatives.

Those initiatives focusing on more narrowly defined child welfare populations are more likely to have funding only from child welfare funding sources, but other initiatives that include some children who are not Title IV-E eligible, for example, "pool funding" from multiple sources.

Each initiative can obtain funding from multiple sources in varying amounts. Table 7 reflects the frequency with which each agency contributes funding rather than their "share" of the total funding.

WAIVERS AND LEGISLATIVE MANDATES SUPPORTING CHANGE

Use of Title IV-E Waivers

Many of the states reporting in 1998 intend to use a Title IV-E waiver to support their proposed initiatives. (The Children's Bureau of the Administration for Children, Youth, and Families grants Title IV-E Demonstration Waivers to permit states to forego compliance with certain guidelines and requirements attached to federal funding established by the Adoption and Child Welfare Assistance Act of 1980. Eighteen states have already been granted Title IV-E waivers.)

Some states are already using Title IV-E child welfare waivers to give the state agency the financial and regulatory flexibility to use federal funding to develop new programs and reduce the rate of growth in expenditures for some "deep end" services. In 1996-7, the following ten states received waivers: California, Delaware, Indiana, Maryland, New York, Illinois, Ohio,

Table 7. Contributing Agencies and Funding Streams

Contributing Agencies	Percentage of Initiatives Receiving Funding from This Source
Child welfare	85%
Medicaid	47%
Mental health	30%
Juvenile justice	19%
Substance abuse	13%
Education	9%
Foundations	6%
Other (TANF, MR/DD, etc.)	17%

Oregon, North Carolina, and Michigan. In 1998, 17 additional states submitted proposals. As of October 1, 1998 eight of these states received waivers: Connecticut, Kansas, Maine, Mississippi, Montana, New Hampshire, New Jersey, and Washington. Of the initiatives described, 47% are located in states that have received a Title IV-E waiver.

As an example of a Title IV-E waiver state, Ohio launched ProtectOhio, a five-year demonstration, in the fall of 1997. Federal and state foster care dollars are combined with county funds and a capitated amount is prepaid to each participating county on a monthly basis; the total budget for Fiscal Year 1999 is $49,015,476.04. The participating counties may serve as their own managed care entity or may contract out and share financial risks with providers or lead agencies. Fourteen of Ohio's 88 counties are participating in the waiver demonstration and many will begin to share risks this year.

Legislation and Regulatory Mandates

For a number of states, the impetus for change came from or was supported by state legislation (see Table 8). Descriptions of legislative or regulatory changes are included in the state profiles. Examples of legislative action include the following:

- Colorado's Senate Bill 97-218 shifted the authority to set rates from the state to the county and Senate Bill 98-165 transformed the way counties are funded and what they can do with their savings. Senate Bill 165 also authorized the counties the discretion for spending up to 5% of savings and allowed the state to replace certain process requirements with outcomes. Legislation also enabled El Paso County to negotiate services and outcomes (not just rates) with providers.

Table 8. Number of Initiatives That Report Legislative or Regulatory Changes

Legislative or Regulatory Changes	Percentage That Report
Legislative	22%
Regulatory	7%

- In 1997, Florida legislation established five model programs to privatize child welfare services by contracting with community-based agencies. During a 1998 legislative session, Florida enacted sweeping legislation that requires the Department of Children and Family Services to develop a plan by July 1, 1999 for the competitive contracting and statewide privatization of foster care and "related services" over the next few years.

- California's Wraparound Services Pilot Program was instituted by Senate Bill 163. The text of the legislation authorizes all counties "to provide children with service alternatives to group home care through the development of expanded family-based services programs. These programs will include individualized or 'wraparound' services."

Integration with Behavioral Health Plans

In most states, managed care or privatization initiatives for the child welfare system have developed with only minimal linkage to managed health or behavioral health plans. There are a few exceptions.

- In Massachusetts, for example, there are two separate public sector programs that have a direct impact on the state's foster care population. Efforts are underway to better coordinate access to services between the two programs. Commonworks is a community-based, residential, specialized foster care and family support program serving more than 1,000 abused and neglected youths who are in the care and custody of the state and require "deep-end" services. The state's managed Medicaid carve-out program, which serves all Medicaid-eligible beneficiaries, including Commonworks children, is managed by ValueOPTIONS. The state also contracts with ValueOPTIONS under a no-risk ASO arrangement to handle billing and reimbursement for authorized services provided by Commonworks' lead agencies and direct service subcontractors. Efforts are underway to improve care coordination for children served by both programs.

- El Paso County, Colorado, is implementing changes that impact the full range of services delivered by the child welfare system. The financing, service delivery, and management of child welfare services are fully integrated with the county's behavioral health managed care plan. Although the county child welfare agency retains primary responsibility for the majority of child welfare functions, the contract with a for-profit managed care entity, Pikes Peak OPTIONS, requires the coordination and delivery of administrative and clinical behavioral health services. Some child welfare and TANF funds were transferred to the behavioral health plan. Pikes Peak OPTIONS will establish risk-sharing arrangements with child welfare agencies for the delivery of certain services.

- Hamilton County, Ohio has a five-year contract, TrueCare, with Magellan Public Solutions, to manage the delivery of behavioral health services to children and families with mental health or substance abuse needs, including those in the child welfare system. The goal is to provide a seamless system of care to an estimated 4,000 children and families using networks of child welfare, substance abuse treatment, and mental health providers. Initially, the existing fee-for-service reimbursement for providers will continue. By the third year, however, it is anticipated that some type of risk-sharing model will be introduced. Side by side with the TrueCare initiative, the county has entered into a case rate contract with a nonprofit agency to manage the care of nearly 300 of the county's most challenging children with expensive service needs. The difficulty will be creating a bridge between the two programs and preventing any shifting of children or costs.

CONCLUSIONS & COMMENTARY

Twenty-nine states reported that they have applied, or are planning to apply, managed care principles and techniques to the management, financing/contracting, or organization and delivery of some or all child welfare services. Significant diversity among initiatives is evidenced in many areas. There are, however, some similarities and trends emerging.

When compared with last year's findings, there is an increase in the number of initiatives that are fully underway or in early implementation, rather than still in the planning stage. The increase appears to be due to several factors, including the approval of Title IV-E waivers, which facilitated more flexible use of funds. In a few states, legislative mandates that were not initiated or anticipated by the public agency provided the stimulus.

Compared to previous years' findings, far more initiatives currently use or propose the use of financial risk-sharing arrangements. Due to uncertainty about accurately pricing child welfare services, it remains to be seen whether these initiatives are adequately funded to ensure high-quality services and the stability of the contract agencies. Many initiatives that include risk-sharing have built in risk adjustment mechanisms to protect against losses that would jeopardize the survival of contractors or the quality of services delivered.

Each year the survey is conducted, public respondents seem more knowledgeable about the potential benefits and the risks associated with managed care. As in past years, public agency administrators do not seem inclined to abandon their missions or mandates to for-profit organizations or nonprofit providers. Instead, they are adapting managed care models to fit the needs of the current system and the unique needs of the population and are limiting the responsibilities being delegated to the private sector. The public sector and the nonprofit providers continue to be the dominant forces shaping managed care and privatization approaches.

Virtually all initiatives report the inclusion of quality assurance requirements and require documentation of outcomes consistent with child welfare values and legal mandates. Nearly half of the initiatives intend to have an independent evaluation conducted. When evaluations are complete, it will be possible to find out whether these experiments resulted in improved system efficiency and effectiveness, and, most importantly, improved outcomes for children and families. The majority of initiatives have placed a premium on the collection of meaningful information about the number of children being served, the types of services being delivered, the costs of services, and whether short-term fiscal and programmatic goals are being met. Perhaps one of the greatest benefits of current efforts will be the ability to generate more accurate data about service need characteristics of the populations, utilization patterns and trends over time, and costs that are linked to the attainment of certain outcomes. This alone may improve a system with historically inadequate and inaccurate data on which to base critical decisions. Yet, despite the information demands of managed care systems and the focus on technology to improve decisionmaking, most current information systems have had difficulty when it comes to tracking information critical to child welfare managed care initiatives. Even highly developed systems created for behavioral health organizations have struggled to comply with child welfare contract demands.

It is important to note that this report is a conservative estimate of what is going on nationwide. While the CWLA Tracking Project's annual survey is quite comprehensive, it proved impossible to get information or confirmation on all projects known to be underway. For example, many of the current Ohio county demonstration sites and several of the other capped counties in Colorado are not yet included. Additionally, some states reported planning for managed care, but were not far enough along in the implementation process to be included in the data analysis. In other instances, states were excluded if their initiatives focused less on child welfare than behavioral health services. Since changes are occurring at a rapid pace, the CWLA Tracking Project database and this report will be updated as new information becomes available.

RESULTS IN BRIEF

Twenty-nine of the 49 states responding to the survey (59%) have one or more initiatives currently underway or planned for implementation within one year. The terms "managed care" or "privatization" might not be terms used by all of the respondents to describe their efforts. Instead, some respondents prefer to report they are using new management tools and funding or contracting strategies to make the system more effective, efficient, and accountable for outcomes.

- *Public purchasers in most of the current initiatives rely upon private nonprofit agencies to manage and deliver services.* Even when certain public functions are shifted to the private sector, however, the public agency continues to be an active partner in decisionmaking at key strategic points. For-profit organizations play a significant role in managing services in only three of the 47 initiatives. Nonprofit agencies, on the other hand, are responsible for case management related to permanency planning in 13 initiatives and for case management related to treatment planning, long-term care decisions, and placement services in 19 initiatives.

- *Seventy-four percent of the initiatives have some financial risk-sharing arrangement in place or planned within the next 12 months.* The public purchaser is much more likely to share risks with nonprofit agencies than with for-profit providers. Risk is currently shared with nonprofit agencies in 29 initiatives and with for-profit organizations in two initiatives. In county-administered states, the public agency may also be at financial risk, through a capped allocation from the state.

- *There is variability in how rates are determined, in the types of risk-sharing arrangements, and in the level of risk borne by contractors.* The most common arrangement is a case rate, often including risk-adjustment mechanisms to limit losses and profits/savings. In most instances, the risk-adjustment mechanism will protect contractors against catastrophic loss. There have been several notable exceptions where the rate was too low, protection too little, and contractors suffered significant losses.

- *Variability in rates proposed for similar initiatives may illustrate how difficult it is to accurately price capitated or case rates in child welfare.* For example, case rates for similar populations and services in different states may vary more than $1,200 per child per month.

- As in previous years, findings indicate that the specific populations vary from one initiative to another with most initiatives targeting children in custody and, specifically, those in out-of-home care settings. *But in 1998, there appears to be an increase in the number of initiatives that are also including children at risk of placement. There are also more plans focusing efforts on the families of children in custody and at risk of placement.*

- *Public agencies report a range of quality assurance mechanisms and reporting requirements to ensure that clients have access to needed care and that contractors are accountable for achieving outcomes consistent with the legal mandates of the system.* In the majority of initiatives, the public purchaser has set performance standards related to access, availability and appropriateness of care and established outcomes related to child and family functioning, and permanency. Contractors are being monitored for progress in meeting specified goals. In some instances, financial bonuses and penalties are being linked to performance in key outcome areas.

- There are many different structural designs for the initiatives. In the most common model, *the public agency is contracting for services in ways that stimulate the development of service delivery networks, often managed by a lead, nonprofit agency.*

- *Since the majority of initiatives have been underway less than 12 months, it is too soon to determine long-term results for the children and families served, or to determine which of the various models holds the most promise for child welfare.*

BEYOND THE DATA: COMMENTARY

Conducting the survey brings new research-related challenges each year. Initially, in 1996 the difficulty was in asking respondents questions about concepts that were new and unfamiliar to them. At that stage, the survey captured interest in managed care and seeds of ideas for initiatives rather than fully developed plans. The results were difficult to assess in terms of validity or reliability. All that could be said was that managed care was being thought about from urban centers to rural America. Beyond talk, there was little concrete enough to analyze.

In 1997, Kansas and Massachusetts and a few other initiatives were actually underway and respondents didn't trip over basic managed care terminology. At that stage, intrigued by Kansas, a majority of states indicated they were moving forward in planning some kind of managed care or privatization initiative. Most were in the early stages of planning and still had little firm notion of how the initiative would be operationalized. Crystal ball predictions about future trends were elusive. In hindsight, states that appeared to be farthest along later ran into financing or political difficulties, stumbled, and have yet to get their plans approved and implemented. Other states that intended to implement large initiatives, scaled back and developed smaller, better designed pilots. On the other hand, states that were barely on the radar screen at the time of the survey moved into high gear and launched initiatives.

Compared to previous years, the results of this year's survey were the easiest to analyze and report. The numbers are more solid; the plans are either underway or on a clear path to being implemented in the near future. There is little doubt now when respondents answer questions that they know what they are being asked. The findings are what they are and there is far less gray to clarify. Yet, like all data, there is ample room for different interpretation.

Placing the Results in Context

It is important to place the 1998 results in context. A few statewide efforts are fully underway, some with expansions into other program areas being planned—including Massachusetts, Kansas, Illinois, and Tennessee. Within the next year, it is likely that Florida will have broadened its privatization pilots to include many more districts. Some county initiatives in county-administered states also affect the entire child welfare population. But most plans are still confined to more narrowly defined populations or smaller geographic areas. While interest in managed care remains high, most public agencies are proceeding with caution.

Nearly all initiatives include the foster care population and the numbers of children and families that are being served in new ways are increasing. But, putting these numbers in perspective we still find that less than 10% of the child welfare population is currently affected by managed care or privatization efforts. Will the numbers continue to grow in future years? Probably, but maybe not at the same accelerated pace we have witnessed this year.

There is a definite increase in the number of initiatives that are attempting to better coordinate care through the formation of integrated provider networks. In some localities, providers took the lead in creating alliances, forming new managed care entities, or merging in the hopes that the purchaser would come. In other instances, the creation of a network was an explicit requirement of an RFP or was undertaken by public agencies working in partnership across systems. Regardless of the impetus, this trend may result in better, more coordinated services for children and families. But, it must be remembered that for the vast majority of children and families, services are still provided by single agencies operating under contracts to deliver a discrete set of services.

Challenges and Concerns

Sweeping changes are most likely to succeed when certain steps are taken to identify and address challenges.

1. A CAREFUL, INCLUSIVE PLANNING PROCESS IS CRITICAL.

A thorough needs assessment and thoughtful planning process will ensure that initiatives are designed to build upon unique strengths and remedy system or community problems.

The survey revealed that a planning process involving various stakeholders, from other public agencies to private providers to the legislature and the courts, preceded most initiatives. What is less clear from the survey, however, is the degree of ownership and level of responsibility stakeholders outside the public agency had in making critical decisions. An open dialogue is critically important in getting needed buy in, building trust, reaching consensus on key design issues, and ensuring that everyone is prepared for their changing roles and responsibilities.

It is clear that additional attention needs to be given to preparing all levels of the organization for the impending changes. Too often, top-down decisions have had to be implemented by ill-prepared staff who had no prior involvement or stake in the success of the plan. Several sites have also had difficulty in meeting goals when the court did not agree with the plan or had not been involved in the planning process. The unique legal and ethical issues involved in providing care to children in custody must be fully explored during planning.

2. THE PROCUREMENT PROCESS MUST BE WELL-MANAGED.

Prior to managed care, public child welfare purchasers have had limited experience in competitively procuring services under risk-based reimbursement systems that are linked to performance. Inexperience has proven embarrassing and costly in several instances. For example, RFPs have been released and bidders have submitted proposals, and then for various reasons the initiative has been cancelled or put on hold. In one instance, the public agency had not secured the funding needed prior to release of the RFP and could not enter into a contract with the winning bidder.

Once a winner has been selected, the public agency must negotiate a contract that includes adequate protections and clearly describes public monitoring and oversight responsibilities. Due to lack of prior experience in these areas, public agencies may need to bring in consultants to assist during RFP development and contract negotiation.

3. IMPLEMENTATION CHALLENGES MUST BE IDENTIFIED AND ADEQUATE TIME AND RESOURCES SHOULD BE COMMITTED TO MEET THE CHALLENGES.

Both public and private agencies must develop new knowledge and skills to succeed under the new initiatives. As the survey revealed, private agencies must prepare to assume new roles, build or buy MIS technology, develop new clinical skills and management tools, learn how to create and manage networks, recruit, hire, and train their staff, and prepare for the chaos inherent during times of rapid growth and upheaval. Staff culture and morale will be affected. For providers operating under risk-share contracts, new risk management skills and tools are essential. Resources must be found to address start up challenges. Yet, as we found in the survey, virtually no initiatives included start-up costs as part of the payment to providers.

Public agencies face equally challenging transition tasks—from having to address the possible reduction in staff, to low morale, to shifting from direct services and developing new contract monitoring and oversight skills. Administrators must also anticipate the challenges in moving to risk-based contracting—from cash flow problems to reporting difficulties.

It is clear that the success of any initiative depends upon adequate funding. It is less clear that states and counties have had the methodologies to accurately price or the ability to adequately fund the system they have created. In managed care, as in most things, you get what you pay for. It may prove unrealistic to have high expectations for service improvement if initiatives are funded at previous or reduced levels. Managed care cannot fix an underfunded system. Some administrators who have lived through the transition acknowledge that additional money should have been allocated to offset some of the initial start-up costs of providers and to sufficiently cushion the public agency against unexpected cash flow difficulties when transitioning to a prospective system of reimbursement.

4. **INITIATIVES MUST INCLUDE INTERNAL AND EXTERNAL EVALUATIONS TO ENSURE THAT CHILDREN AND FAMILIES ARE BEING WELL-SERVED AND FISCAL AND PROGRAMMATIC GOALS ARE BEING MET.**

A lot of things are being tried at the same time—from changing reimbursement methods, to creating provider networks, to changing how services are managed. Even when results appear positive, it takes a thorough evaluation to assess which of the changes had the greatest impact. This requires a significant investment of time and resources. Too often, purchasers have not adequately planned or funded the research that will be needed. At best, dollars may have been deducted from the service budget to pay for internal or external evaluations. With so much at risk, it is critical that states and counties support the independent evaluations needed to determine what does and does not work.

It is equally important to have the flexibility to continuously redesign elements of the initiative in response to internal monitoring of data. What is initially conceived may not prove to be the best model. Initiatives should be continuously evaluated, changed, and reassessed over time to ensure that children and families are being well-served.

Table 9. The 29 States at a Glance

State/Initiative	Approximate Annual # of Children Served	Types of Model	Financing & Approximate Rates	Year Started
Arizona				
Privatization Service Delivery	2,000	Lead agency	Case rate to be determine (TBD)	1999 TBD
Family Builders	6,000	Lead agency (8)	Case rate $3,500	1998
California				
Project Heartbeat	TBD	Public interagency and lead agencies	Case rate $3,300	1999
San Diego Wraparound Services (SB 163)	TBD	Public	Capped allocation to county with county match at RCL13--$4,720	1998
Colorado				
El Paso Protection	3,286	Public	Capped at $34 million	1998
El Paso/Pikes Peak OPTIONS	300-500 foster care children	MCO	Capitated at $5 million, to share risk with providers FY 1999	1998
Connecticut				
Continuum of Care Model	120	Lead agency (2)	Case rate, about $48,000 for 15 months, plus bonus tied to performance	1999
Delaware				
CPS Low-Risk Intervention	165	Public contracts with single agencies	Case rate with 2 providers, $1,250-$1,500, with a $250 bonus (other 2 providers FFS)	1998
Florida				
District 4	350	Lead agency	No risk, $3 million FY98, risk in 1999	1997
District 1	150	Single agency	No risk, FY98, share risk in 1999 $1 million	1992
District 8	400	Lead agency	Capitated at $4 million over 18 months	1997
District 13	90	Single agency	Case rate of $15,200 FY98, now capitated	1997
Georgia				
MATCH (Multi-Agency)	660	Public interagency collaborative	$46 million approx. annual budget	1994
Hawaii				
Ohana Family Conferencing	100	Public agencies and provider networks	Bonuses and penalties are linked to the attainment of outcome measures/performance-based contracts	

Conclusions & Commentary 47

Table 9. The 29 States at a Glance (continued)

State/Initiative	Approximate Annual # of Children Served	Types of Model	Financing & Approximate Rates	Year Started
Illinois Performance contracts	35,850	Public contracts with single agencies	FY99 $334 million, FFS with penalties and bonuses	1997, expanded in 1999
Indiana Child Welfare Demonstration	4,000	Public interagency agreement	Case rate of no more than $9,000 per child $20.4 million for 24 months	1998
Kansas Family Preservation	2,472	Lead agency	Case rate $3,719 for 12 months	1997
Adoption	1,053	Lead agency	Case rate $14,746 for 18 months postfinalization	1997
Foster Care	4,430	Lead agency	Case rate $14,022 for 12 months postreunification	1997
Kentucky Quality Care Pilot	100	Public contract with single agency	FFS, with case rate within a year FY99 $3 million	1999
Maryland Baltimore City	1,000	Lead agency	Case rate for 3 years, not yet established, not more than $3,500 per month	1999
Massachusetts Commonworks	1,100	Lead agency (6) & ASO	Lead agencies have case rate of $4,447; ASO no risk, $2.2 million	1996, with risk introduced in 1998, $45 million total
Family Based	TBD	Lead agency	No risk, phase in risk, $31 million FY99	1999

Conclusions & Commentary   49

Table 9. The 29 States at a Glance (continued)

State/Initiative	Approximate Annual # of Children Served	Types of Model	Financing & Approximate Rates	Year Started
Michigan				
Michigan Families	Minimum 120 (from 6 sites)	Public/collaborative network	Case of $1,500 per month per case for IV-E eligible, plus other state and local $	1999
Permanency-focused reimbursement	650	Single agencies	Performance-based: $1,700 initial, $14.94 per day, $1,500 for meeting permanency goal or TPR, bonus of $730 for good outcome at 6 months postplacement	1997
Adoption contracting	None provided	Single agency	Performance-based, diminishing rate over time	1992
Minnesota				
Hennepin County collaborative	800	Local collaborative	Pooled funding; $7 million budget projected for FY99	1998
Missouri				
Interdepartmental Children's Services	500 (3-year contract, 1,500 total	Lead agency & ASO	Lead agency has case rate of $3,200 per child, per month, with bonus post-enrollment; ASO is no risk, fixed fee. Total funding of $42 million for the next 3 years	1999
New York				
Neighborhood-based Borough of the Bronx	27,500 families	Lead agencies	$5,000 per family for up to 18 months	1999
North Carolina				
Buncombe County	3,403	Public	Capped allocation to county, risk share with providers within a year	1998

Table 9. The 29 States at a Glance (continued)

State/Initiative	Approximate Annual # of Children Served	Types of Model	Financing & Approximate Rates	Year Started
Ohio				
Crawford County	22	MCO (for-profit agency)	Capped to county, MCO paid case rate $38,500 for 6 months postreunification	1998
Cuyahoga County	Up to 500 (192 families)	Lead agency	Case rate TBD	1999
Franklin County	1,000 (500 families)	Lead agency (2)	Case rate & penalties linked to performance Budget for FY99 is approx. $7 million	1998
Hamilton County Creative Connections	286 (200 families)	Lead agency	Case rate $3,130.29 per member per month, $12 million allocated for FY99	1999
Hamilton County TrueCare Partnership	3,200	MCO	No risk with MCO, penalties and bonuses, provider risk planned for this FY $14 million project for FY99	1998
Lorain County Integrated Services	23	Lead agency	No risk Year 1, risk in Year 2	1998
Oklahoma				
Children's Services Initiative	3,700 children, 2,500 families	Lead agency/network	No risk Year 1, up to $3,000 per family, with up to $400 in goods; case rate Year 2, perhaps $400 per month for up to 6 months $7.2 million plus Medicaid	1998
Pennsylvania				
Berkserve	30	Lead agency with MSO	No risk in Year 1, case rate in Year 2	1997
South Carolina				
Privatized adoption	200-250	Private, nonprofit agencies	FFS, performance-based schedule of payments, maximum of $13,000 per child; $15,700 per sibling group	1998

Table 9. The 29 States at a Glance (continued)

State/Initiative	Approximate Annual # of Children Served	Types of Model	Financing & Approximate Rates	Year Started
Tennessee				
Nonresidential network	TBD	Lead agency	TBD	1999
Continuum of care contracts	2,500	Lead agency	Case rate	1997
Texas				
Project PACE	200	Lead agency	Fixed daily rate of $72.40 per day, regardless of level of care; case rate possible in later years	1998
Utah				
Residential contracting restructuring	1,800	Public contracts with single providers	Negotiate fixed daily rate within the year, range from $56-$227 per day; projected budget for FY99 is $45 million	1999
Washington				
Capitated payment for children with special needs Title IV-E, Spokane County	380	Regional collaborative networks	Capped allocation	1999

TABLE 9. THE 29 STATES AT A GLANCE (CONTINUED)

State/Initiative	Approximate Annual # of Children Served	Types of Model	Financing & Approximate Rates	Year Started
West Virgnia				
Region IV Foster Care Pilot	400	Lead agency/network	Case rate TBD	1999
Wisconsin				
Milwaukee Case Management	Not reported	Lead agency in 3 sites	Fixed amount per site with bonuses and penalties; total amount awarded to the 3 sites was $10,590,520	1998
Wraparound Milwaukee*	600		Case rate $3,300 and penalties; total amount awarded to the 3 sites was $10,590,520	1996
SafeNow Safety	2,220 children (740 families) 1,062 children & 354 families last year, 3,378 children & 1,126 families projected for upcoming year	Lead agency	TBD; $6,286,940 has been allocated for the upcoming year; $3,447,074 was used during the first year	1998

* Wraparound Milwaukee was not included in the analysis, but the number of children was incorporated into the total number of children served.

1998 STATE PROFILES
Managed Care and Privatization Initiatives

ARIZONA

Arizona has two initiatives in the child welfare arena: 1) the Service Privatization Delivery Project, and 2) Family Builders. Family Builders is underway and the privatization initiative is in the planning stage.

Privatization Service Delivery Project

Arizona is exploring the feasibility of expanding privatization efforts and contracting with lead agencies for coordinated, outcome-driven services to improve current performance.

Goals. Central goals include decreasing length of stay in out-of-home care, improving client outcomes, increasing permanency in the shortest time possible, and increasing the safety and well-being of children.

Populations Served. Populations eligible for this initiative include all children in child welfare custody, adoptive families and children with adoption as the permanency goal, and families of children in state custody. The State estimates that 2,000 children (1,500 families) will receive services.

Services. The current plan is for the initiative to be implemented in phases, with separate contracts for adoption, out-of-home care, and in-home services. All current services may eventually be privatized with the exception of child protective services (CPS) intake and investigation. The state intends to begin the implementation process with adoption services and continue to study the feasibility of including other services.

Quality and Outcomes. Reports from families and providers, focus groups of stakeholders and customers, standardized assessments, and utilization, cost, and performance data from a management information (MIS) tracking system will be used to monitor quality requirements and outcomes in the following areas:

- Specific system performance indicators related to program effectiveness;
- Specific criteria related to appropriateness of services, based on standardized protocols;
- Consumer satisfaction requirement, based on child and family data;
- Outcomes related to achievement of permanency planning goals;
- Outcomes related to recidivism/reentry;
- Requirements to adhere to professional standards or licensing requirements;
- Credentialing requirements for individual providers;
- Specific criteria or standards related to cultural competence of providers or managed care entities; and
- An independent evaluation of the initiative/demonstration.

Roles and Responsibilities. The state child welfare administration will retain primary responsibility for determining Title IV-E or Medicaid eligibility, ongoing utilization management, contracting with a lead agency, tracking outcomes and system performance indicators, and billing and reimbursement. Under a risk-share contract, a lead agency/provider will have primary responsibility for gatekeeping for certain care, creating provider networks, case management related to permanency planning, treatment planning, long-term care determination, and placement services, and data collection to meet state and federal reporting requirements.

Financial Arrangements. Arizona's initiative will be financed by state-appropriated funds and, when applicable, Title IV-E and other federal funds. The state plans to request a Title IV-E waiver, but has not begun the process. The state is not certain what other legislative or regulatory changes will be required. The state plans to share risk with lead agencies, using a case rate for adoption-related services, during the upcoming year. The case rate will be based on a historical review of the cost of contracted adoption-related services. The amount of the case rate, whether the contract will include a risk adjustment mechanism, and limitations regarding any savings/ profits accumulated by providers have not been determined.

Family Builders

This demonstration project provides family support and preservation services through collaborative partnerships between the state's CPS agency, community social service agencies, and other community organizations. The project was approved by the state legislature. Two pilot sites, Maricopa and Pima Counties, were selected in January 1998. These counties represent approximately 75% of the state's child welfare population. The state has contracted with eight providers to deliver services. One provider, Catholic Social Services, provides services in both counties. The other seven providers include Arizona Baptist Children's Services, Arizona's Children Association, Black Family and Child Services, Inc., Child and Family Resources collaborators, CARENOW Collaborator's, Marana Unified School District, and Our Town Family Center.

Goals. The central goals are preventing or reducing the incidence of child abuse, redirecting public CPS staff to handle high-risk cases, and improving family and child functioning.

Populations Served. Low-risk CPS cases are voluntarily served. The initiative aims to serve approximately 6,000 families each year. During the first six months of the initiative 2,000 reports were referred, 659 assessments were conducted, and 555 service plans were completed.

Services Provided. Family Builders provides individualized services including family strengths assessment and support. As required by legislation (House Bill 2256), the following services are available to families: assessment, case management, child care, housing search and relocation, parenting skills training, supportive intervention and guidance counseling, transportation, emergency services, intensive family preservation services, parent aide services, respite services, and shelter with parental consent.

The state reports that case management is the service provided most frequently, followed by counseling, parent aide, and transportation.

Quality and Outcomes. Reports from families and providers; standardized assessments; pre- and post-tests; utilization, cost, and performance data from MIS tracking systems; analysis from an automated system for child protective services designed to identify subsequent reports; and monitoring reports from quarterly site visits will be used to monitor quality requirements and outcome measures in the following areas:

- Specific system performance indicators related to program effectiveness (reduction in risk and analysis of subsequent CPS region),
- Specific criteria related to cost (the use of a three-tiered case rate),
- Specific criteria related to access/availability of services and utilization patterns (certain services are mandated to be available to all families referred, based on their needs),
- Consumer satisfaction requirement (client satisfaction survey is conducted),
- Outcomes related to child and family functioning (the Family Risk Scale and Family Assessment Scale are used to assess),
- Outcomes related to recidivism/reentry (no more than 10% referred with substantiated CPS reports),
- Requirements to adhere to professional standards or licensing requirements (required in contract with providers), and
- An independent evaluation of the initiative (being evaluated by the Office of the Auditor General.

Roles and Responsibilities. The state agency issued an RFP and entered contracts with nonprofit lead agencies who are responsible for creating community-based provider networks, subcontracting with providers, accepting initial referrals, conducting family assessments, data tracking, and program evaluation. The state agency will ensure payment and monitor the lead agencies for contract compliance, quality, and program evaluation.

Financing/Contracting. Legislation passed in 1997 that designated $800,000 for fiscal year 1998. A Senate Bill was passed during the Second Special Session that appropriated an additional $3,555,600 for fiscal year 1998. Thus, the total appropriation for fiscal year 1998 was $4,355,600, $8 million has been appropriated for fiscal year 1999.

The state shares financial risk with nonprofit lead agencies through a case rate of $3,500 per family. The three-tiered payment schedule pays the following amounts for each of the following levels of service: $100 for referral, $250 for assessment, and $3,500 for the completion of the service plan.

California

California reported three statewide initiatives in which counties may elect to participate: 1) Senate Bill 163 Wraparound Services Pilot, 2) California's Title IV-E Waiver Demonstration Project, and 3) the California Structured Decision-Making (SDM) Project. Senate Bill 163 uses managed care tools and shares financial risk with counties.

California is a county-administered state and, as such, also has a variety of initiatives developed and implemented by different counties.

Senate Bill 163 Wraparound Services Pilot Program

The state legislature, state child welfare agency, state mental health agency, nonprofit private providers, children and families (consumers), and juvenile and family court were involved the planning process. Senate Bill 163, Chapter 795 established implementation and compliance standards for counties to be eligible for participation in the initiative.

Goals. Central principles of the initiative include a commitment to unconditional comprehensive care that is individualized, community-based, culturally competent, needs-driven, family-centered, and child-focused. Service plans should be strength-based, emphasize normalization, and encourage parent ownership and involvement.

The central goal of the initiative is to increase the ability of counties to provide wraparound services to children as an alternative to group care. Funding flexibility increases the ability of counties to provide the individualized, intensive wraparound services packages necessary to maintain children in, or return them to, family settings. Increased use of natural community-based resources is central to the success of the initiative.

Populations Served. Eligible populations include 1) children adjudicated as dependents or wards of the juvenile court who are, or would be, placed in a group home licensed by the Department at a rate classification level of 12 or above, and 2) children who would be voluntarily placed in out-of-home care pursuant to Section 7572.5 of the Government Code.

Services. Services could include case management, permanency planning with families, treatment foster care, group care, residential care/treatment, psychiatric hospitalization, mental health and substance abuse treatment services, wraparound services, and respite care.

Quality and Outcomes. Service plans are evaluated systematically for outcome measures. Reports from families, providers, and schools, and standardized assessments will be used to monitor quality requirements and outcomes. Additionally, although the initiative does not include a requirement for independent evaluation of the programs, it does require that counties evaluate their pilot projects, prepare interim and final evaluations, and submit them to the California Department of Social Services and the California legislature. The initiative has incorporated and will continue to develop quality requirements and specific outcome indicators in the following areas:

- Specific system performance indicators related to program effectiveness,
- Specific criteria related to cost (costs are limited to state foster care funds and county match of RCL 13 Level [$4,720] minus the cost of any concurrent out-of-home placement costs),
- Specific criteria related to access/availability of services and utilization patterns,
- Criteria related to appropriateness of services (services are driven by individualized strength-based family-centered assessment and planning process, fewer children will be in high-end group care/institutions, and length-of-stay in group home care will be reduced),
- Consumer satisfaction requirement (county plans must include processes for supporting a high level of family involvement and measuring satisfaction),
- Outcomes related to child functioning,
- Outcomes related to family functioning,
- Outcomes related to achievement of permanency planning goals (more children will be in a permanent, safe and stable family setting),
- Credentialing requirements for individual providers (an accreditation process for lead wraparound provider agencies is being developed),
- Criteria or standards related to cultural competence of providers or managed care entities (counties must address cultural competence as part of their wraparound plans),
- An independent evaluation of the initiative/demonstration (counties are required to evaluate their pilot projects, prepare and interim and final evaluation and submit them to CDSS and the legislature), and
- Interagency collaboration and satisfaction will increase.

Roles and Responsibilities. The county child welfare agency retains primary responsibility for determining Title IV-E or Medicaid eligibility, contracting with providers, billing and reimbursement, and creating provider networks. Additionally, this initiative involves the use of individualized family teams (consisting of family members, multiple agencies, and informal resources) that will collaborate with the county child welfare agency and assume responsibility for the following functions: tracking outcomes and system performance indicators, case management, and collecting data to meet state and federal reporting requirements.

Financial Arrangements. The initiative is intended to be cost neutral. The state does not provide new funding, but allows flexible use of state foster care funds with a match from the county for services. Costs are limited to state foster care funds and county match at RCL 13 Level of $4,720, minus the cost of any concurrent out-of-home placement costs. Savings obtained through more effective utilization of community resources will be reinvested in prevention, early intervention, and other services to at-risk children and families.

San Diego: Project Heartbeat

Project Heartbeat is a multisystem effort to create an integrated system of care for children with SED or behavioral health needs and their families. The planning and implementation process is involving the family sector, the public sector, and the private sector. When completely implemented Project Heartbeat will change the management, financing, and delivery of services across multiple systems.

Goals. Central goals include allowing providers the flexibility to provide individualized and accessible care, "pooling funding" to create a more seamless system of care, improving family and child functioning, and increasing the availability of front-end services in order to limit unnecessary residential placements.

Populations Served. When completely implemented Project Heartbeat may serve all Medi-Cal eligible children, children with SED, regardless of whether or not they are in custody, and families of children in or at risk of entering custody.

According to the "Health Care Reform Tracking Project: Special Analysis on Child Welfare Managed Care Reform Initiatives" [Schulzinger et al. 1999], the initial target population will include those children in custody or at risk of entering custody.

Services. Project Heartbeat intends to use wraparound approaches to planning and delivering individualized care to children and families. Services will include the full array of out-of-home care options and in-home and community services.

Quality and Outcomes. The initiative will monitor outcomes and quality requirements in the following areas:

- Outcomes related to child and family functioning,
- Consumer satisfaction requirement,
- Specific criteria related to appropriateness of services,
- Specific criteria related to access/availability of services and utilization patterns, and
- Specific criteria related to cost.

Roles and Responsibilities. Roles and responsibilities are still being defined. It is clear that the three sectors—the client (child and family), the private agencies, and the multiple public sector agencies—will share major tasks. It is likely that an administrative service organization (ASO) will be selected to develop and manage an automated MIS to track clients, track system performance and client outcomes, collect data to meet federal and state reporting requirements, to assist in creating provider networks, and managing claims adjudication and reimbursement.

An ASO will have primary responsibility for the following functions: tracking outcomes and system performance indicators, data collection for the purpose of meeting state and federal reporting requirements, billing and reimbursement, and providing administrative support services to provider networks.

The public agencies and Project Heartbeat still have to determine how pre-authorization, gatekeeping for certain care, contracting with providers, and case management related to permanency planning, treatment planning, long-term care determination, placement services, and for behavioral health services for the family will be managed.

Financial Arrangements. When fully implemented, the county projects that a budget of approximately $60 million will be allocated for this initiative. Annie E. Casey, the California Endowment, and a CMHS grant provided support for the planning phase of the initiative. Medi-Cal, Title IV-E, mental health, education will contribute funding for implementation.

The timetable for full implementation is still uncertain.

COLORADO

Colorado is a state-supervised/county-administered system. In 1997, the state legislature authorized the state to select three pilot counties to participate in a capped allocation managed care model for managing and delivering child welfare services. After an RFP process, the state selected Boulder, Jefferson, and Mesa Counties as the initial pilot sites. At the same time, a fourth county, El Paso, was also involved in developing a number of initiatives that use managed care techniques. The state legislature has expanded the initiative to implement three new pilots. El Paso, Pueblo, and Arapahoe Counties have been selected and implementation is underway.

Colorado's Capped Allocation to Six Counties

Goals. Central goals include ensuring more efficient use of limited resources, increasing permanency in the shortest time possible, increasing the safety and well-being of children, and controlling, predicting, and limiting costs.

Populations Served. In five of the six counties, populations eligible for this initiative include children in custody, children served by child welfare agencies who are not in custody, families of children in custody, families of children at risk of being in custody, developmentally disabled children, and children and families involved with the juvenile justice system. In Boulder County, the sixth pilot site, the previous populations are eligible, but service delivery is limited to adolescents.

Services. Services include case management, child protective service intake, emergency shelter, family preservation and support services, day treatment, permanency planning with families, kinship care, family foster care, treatment foster care, and group and residential care.

Quality and Outcomes. The state requires pilot counties to participate in monthly problem-solving meetings and dedicate ten hours per year to technology development as mechanisms for ensuring quality. The counties rely on reports from families, standardized assessment, quarterly reports, and utilization, cost, and performance data from MIS tracking systems to track outcome and quality requirements in the following areas:

- Specific system performance indicators related to program effectiveness,
- Criteria related to appropriateness of services,
- Development of Level of Care criteria or clinical protocols,
- Outcomes related to child functioning (the state will use the North Carolina assessment tool as a pre- and post-test; CAFAS is being considered for children older than 12),

- Outcomes related to family functioning (the state will use the North Carolina assessment tool next year as a pre- and post-test),
- Requirements to adhere to professional standards or licensing,
- Specific criteria or standards related to cultural competence of providers or managed care entities (counties are scored based on what they require of themselves in this area), and
- An independent evaluation of the initiative/demonstration, Senate Bill 165 provides the funding for the evaluation.

Financial Arrangements. State and county child welfare agencies, county mental health agencies, Medicaid, and county juvenile justice agencies provide funding for the initiative. The percentage of the total budget provided by each source varies for each of the pilot sites, however. A Medicaid mental health waiver provides funding flexibility that contributes to the success of partnerships and collaboration. A Title IV-E waiver proposal is being submitted to further increase the flexibility of funding streams.

The state provides each county with a capped allocation, but risk-sharing arrangements between the county agency and providers vary by county. A cap on potential retained savings requires that any savings above 5% be reinvested into the child welfare system.

Senate Bills 97-218 and 98-165 were central to the creation of the state's managed care initiatives because they alter the way counties are funded and enable them to retain savings. Senate Bill 97-218 shifted the authority and responsibility for rate setting from the state to the county. Senate Bill 98-165 waived the process requirements, refocused the program on outcomes, and authorized counties to spend funds on private/independent evaluations.

Roles and Responsibilities. The state child welfare agency assumes primary responsibility for the creation of Level of Care/service system criteria, tracking outcome and system performance indicators to meet the quality assurance oversight function, and collecting data to meet state and federal reporting requirements.

The county child welfare agency has primary responsibility for the development and delivery of child welfare services, including determining Title IV-E or Medicaid eligibility, pre-authorizing care, gatekeeping for care, ongoing utilization management, case management related to permanency planning, treatment planning, long-term care determination, and placement services, creating provider networks, billing and reimbursement, and collecting data to meet state and federal reporting requirements. The county child welfare agencies also have responsibility for the case management of mental health and substance abuse treatment for families involved in the child welfare system.

The counties are free to enter into performance-based, or other risk-share arrangements with nonprofit providers and, if they desire, contract with a MCE for certain administrative functions.

Two initiatives in El Paso County are highlighted. The Managed Care Institute plans to release a description of all six pilot sites during the upcoming year.

El Paso County's Protection System

This countywide initiative is currently implementing changes in the management, delivery, and financing of the full range of child welfare services. The Board of County Commissioners, state legislature, state and county child welfare agencies, state Medicaid agency, state and county mental health agencies, state and county alcohol and drug abuse agencies, nonprofit private providers, consumers, juvenile and family courts, local foundations, and foster parents were involved in the planning process.

Goals. Central goals include improving client outcomes, improving quality of services, increasing permanency in the shortest time possible, and increasing the safety and well-being of children.

Populations Served. All children in custody, including those in out-of-home care, are eligible for this initiative. During the past year, approximately 3,100 children from 2,300 families were served. The county expects a 6% increase in the number of children and families who will receive services during the upcoming year.

Services. Services include case management, child protective services intake and investigations, emergency shelter, family preservation and support, day treatment, permanency planning with families, kinship care, family foster care, treatment foster care, group care, residential care/treatment, psychiatric hospitalization, adoption recruitment and services, postadoption subsidies and support, juvenile justice, behavioral health treatment, wraparound services, respite care, and independent living services.

Quality and Outcomes. Reports from families and providers, standardized assessments, pre- and post-tests, and utilization, cost, and performance data from MIS tracking systems are used to measure quality requirements and outcomes in the following areas:

- System performance indicators related to program effectiveness (outcomes related to child safety),
- Criteria related to access/availability of services and utilization patterns,
- Specific criteria related to appropriateness of services,
- Development of Level of Care criteria or clinical protocols,
- Consumer satisfaction sampling,
- Outcomes related to child functioning,
- Outcomes related to family functioning,
- Outcomes related to achievement of permanency planning goals,
- Requirements to adhere to professional standards or licensing requirements,
- Credentialing requirements for individual providers, and
- Specific criteria/standards related to cultural competence of providers (staffing patterns reflect the population that will receive services).

Although the initiative does not currently include an independent evaluation, as a result of the statewide legislation that was mentioned earlier, it will be required to add one.

Roles and Responsibilities. When child welfare services are being delivered, the county child welfare agency will retain primary responsibility for the following functions: CPS investigation and assessment, determination of Title IV-E or Medicaid eligibility, pre-authorizing and gatekeeping for care, ongoing utilization management, contracting with a private managed care entity (Pikes Peak OPTIONS L.L.C.) for behavioral health services, contracting with providers and creating provider networks, tracking outcomes and system performance indicators, case management related to permanency planning and placement services, billing and reimbursement, and collecting data for the purpose of meeting state and federal reporting requirements.

Financial Arrangements. The county child welfare agency has assumed risk in the form of a capped allocation for child welfare services. The county child welfare agencies negotiated rates with providers. During the past year the budget was $32 million, this is expected to increase to $34 million during the upcoming fiscal year. Fifteen percent of this funding is local and the other 85% represents state and federal funds.

El Paso County/Pikes Peak OPTIONS Behavioral Health Care Network for Foster Care Populations

El Paso County's behavioral health care initiative for the child welfare population involves the used of a 1915(b) Medicaid waiver. This waiver was crucial because it allowed the county to double funds for behavioral health services by ensuring that it receives a match from the federal government.

Population. Serving between 300-500 children in the foster care system with identified SED needs and the families of children in foster care.

Financial Arrangements. Child welfare, mental health, and Medicaid agencies contribute funding to this initiative, providing $2.6 million for year one and $5 million per year for following years.

Roles and Responsibilities. The county agency determines eligibility and refers children and families to the MCE under contract with the county agency, Pikes Peak OPTIONS L.L.C., for services.

Under a risk-share contract, Pikes Peak OPTIONS L.L.C. assumes primary responsibility for the following functions for the child welfare population: creating medical necessity or service necessity criteria, pre-authorizing or gatekeeping for care, ongoing utilization management, contracting with providers and creating provider networks, tracking outcomes and system performance indicators, case management related to treatment planning, and collecting data for the purpose of meeting state and federal reporting requirements.

The aforementioned for-profit managed care entity assumes full risk for the provision of behavioral health services to the child welfare population. The MCE intends to contract with providers using a case rate.

Connecticut

Connecticut has recently been awarded a Title IV-E waiver and will soon begin implementing its demonstration, the Continuum of Care Service Delivery Model. The waiver allows the state to establish capitated payment systems in two pilot sites. A single lead agency in each site will coordinate all offered services through a network of providers under a case rate that covers 12 months of services and three months of follow-up.

The state also described its efforts to develop an outcomes measurement system, and revise administrative case reviews.

Continuum of Care Service Delivery Model

Changes in how services are managed, delivered, and contracted are currently being implemented in this small demonstration project as part of

Connecticut's Title IV-E Waiver. The Governor's Office, state legislature, state child welfare agency, Department of Education, state juvenile justice agency, nonprofit private providers, and consumers were involved in planning this initiative.

The Connecticut Department of Children and Families (DCF) released an RFP for this initiative and has chosen two lead service agencies (LSAs)—the Middlesex Hospital and Klingberg Family Centers, Inc., the fiduciary for the Hartford consortium.

Goals. Central goals include decreasing length of stay in out-of-home care, providing individualized and accessible care, maintaining children in their communities, and improving client outcomes (specifically, increasing children's satisfaction with services, improving their behavioral health, and reducing substantiated allegation of child abuse and neglect).

Population Served. Populations eligible for this initiative include all children between the ages of 7 and 15 who have been authorized for placement in a residential treatment center or group home. Each lead service agency will serve a total of 60 children. An additional 60 youth will serve as a control group.

Services. Services include evaluations, case management, emergency shelter, family preservation and support services, day treatment, family foster care, treatment foster care, group care, residential care/treatment, mental health and substance abuse treatment, respite care, independent living/community life skills training, crisis intervention, extended day treatment, individual and family counseling, aftercare, and parent aide and support.

Quality and Outcomes. Reports from families and providers, standardized assessments, and utilization, cost, and performance data from MIS tracking systems will be used to monitor quality requirements and outcomes in the following areas:

- System performance indicators related to program effectiveness (a significant reduction in the length of stay for youth who are placed in a long-term group care setting),

- Specific criteria related to cost,

- Criteria related to access/availability of services and utilization patterns (the lead agency must demonstrate the capacity of all network providers to deliver all required services in the targeted DCF region, and the lead agency must propose a time frame for the period between the receipt of the referral from DCF and the completion of an individualized treatment plan with specific services identified),

- Criteria related to appropriateness of services (to significantly reduce the average length of stay for youth who are placed in a group care setting, reduce the number of children who enter long-term group care, and divert the number of children who enter long-term group care),

- DCF and the lead service agencies will jointly develop Level of Care criteria and credentialing standards,

- Consumer satisfaction requirement (improve satisfaction with services received by children and families, the lead service agency will establish and facilitate a consumer/parent advisory board),

- Outcomes related to child functioning (pre- and post-test improvement demonstrated by a standardized behavioral measure),

- Outcomes related to family functioning,

- Outcomes related to recidivism/reentry (demonstrate that clients will remain in a stable placement for six months following the discontinuation of services),

- Requirements to adhere to professional standards or licensing requirements,

- Credentialing requirements for individual providers (the lead planning agency must document that all network providers and subcontractors are licensed and certified by appropriate agencies and are in compliance with federal, state, and local statutes, regulations, policies and procedures),

- Accreditation of agencies/facilities according to national standards,

- Criteria or standards related to cultural competence of providers or managed care entities (the lead planning agency must describe how the contractor plans to assure that culturally competent services reflecting the diverse socioeconomic, ethnic and racial composition of clients are provided. This description should include program staffing, bilingual and bicultural services offered by network providers or subcontractors), and

- An independent evaluation of the initiative/demonstration. The DCF and the lead service agency will both work with an independent project evaluator.

Roles and Responsibilities. The state child welfare agency will retain primary responsibility for determining Title IV-E or Medicaid eligibility, pre-authorizing and gatekeeping for care, contracting with a lead agency functioning as a managed care entity, case management, and collecting data to meet state and federal reporting requirements.

Under a risk-share contract, a not-for-profit lead service agency will assume primary responsibility for ongoing utilization management, contracting with providers, creating provider networks, tracking outcomes and system performance indicators, and billing and reimbursement.

Financial Arrangements. It is likely that funding for this initiative will be drawn from various sources (child welfare, mental health, juvenile justice, etc.) and that additional flexibility will be provided by the Title IV-E waiver that was recently approved by the federal government. Final financing arrangements have not been agreed upon. However, the state does plan to share financial risks with a not-for-profit lead service agency. Although rates have not yet been established, the state reports that it expects to use a case rate of approximately $48,000 per child for 15 months for all services covered under the initiative. The final case rate will be based on annualized average per diem costs for residential and group home care. The state also plans to include a financial bonus (up to 10%) based on successful and timely completion of treatment plan. The contract will include a risk adjustment mechanism of approximately 10% and limit the potential profits of the lead agency to 10% of the case rate.

DELAWARE

The state reported two initiatives. The first is targeted towards low-risk CPS families and the second is designed to assist families barred from TANF. (Delaware also has a Title IV-E waiver to provide enhanced services to substance-abusing caretakers and to support assisted guardianship for children in stable foster care placements for whom reunification or adoption are not possible. The demonstration does not involve any financial risk-sharing or use of managed care tools.)

Delaware's CPS Low-Risk Intervention

Goals. Central goals include ensuring more efficient use of limited resources, increasing the safety and well-being of children, maintaining children in their communities, and diverting low-risk CPS cases out of the formal CPS system.

Populations Served. Populations eligible for this initiative include all families investigated and identified as low risk. The initiative served 165 families in the past year.

Services. The initiative includes the delivery of a range of therapeutic and family support services.

Quality and Outcomes. Pre- and post-tests, and utilization, cost, and performance data will be used to monitor quality requirements and outcomes in the following areas:

- System performance indicators related to program effectiveness (a 25% reduction of risk for 75% of families completing the program, based on CWLA Family Well-Being Scales),
- Outcomes related to family functioning based on CWLA Family Well-Being Scales, and
- Outcomes related to recidivism/reentry (less than 10% re-reported).

Roles and Responsibilities. The state child welfare agency retains primary responsibility for contracting with providers and tracking outcomes and system performance indicators.

Two nonprofit providers, under a risk-shared contract, will have primary responsibility for case management services and child protective treatment services. Two additional contractors will provide services under no-risk arrangements.

Financial Arrangements. Funding for this initiative is provided by the state child welfare agency. The current budget is $250,000, this is 1.7% of the total child welfare funds. The state does not plan to increase the initiative's budget or the number of families served in the upcoming year.

There are four contractors. Two contractors will continue to operate under a fee-for-service system until they have compiled sufficient data for determining a case rate. The other two contractors will operate under a financial risk-sharing arrangement that includes both case rates and financial bonuses. The amount of the case rate can range from $1,250 to $1,500 dollars and is awarded in a lump sum at the completion of assessment, prior to case planning and service delivery. A $250 bonus is available to providers contingent upon successful case closure within six months and no reentry for a year.

Florida

In 1996 the Florida legislature mandated that the Department of Children and Families establish model privatization pilots in different districts of the state. The deadline for implementing provider contracts was January 1, 1997. Those pilots were intended to strengthen "the support and commitment of communities to the reunification of families and care of children and their families, and result in increased efficiencies and accountability." Pilots were implemented in four districts: District 1, 4, 8, and 13. Each of these initial pilots is summarized below.

The legislation afforded each pilot great latitude in determining the focus and scope of their respective initiatives. In designing the programs, the projects in Districts 4, 8, and 13 each applied various elements of managed care in an effort to improve outcomes and increase system efficiencies. For example, in District 4, the provider developed a utilization review process to help allocate limited resources across cases. In District 8, a network of providers was created with a lead agency, the YMCA, managing the contracts and the care. District 8 also operates under a capitated arrangement—the same amount of money is received regardless of the number of children and families served.

The state is tracking and monitoring outcomes across all privatization pilots. Since most are relatively new, the independent evaluation has not yet been completed. The state is considering a number of variables, including the following:

- Child safety,
- Improved child and family functioning,
- Reduced placements after entering care,
- Shortened length of stay,
- Achievement of the permanency plan,
- Increase family involvement/stability,
- Increase use of less restrictive placements,
- Improved preparation for independent living,
- Improved client satisfaction, and
- Recognized cost efficiencies.

More recently, legislation was passed requiring the Department to develop a plan by July 1, 1999 for the competitive contracting and *statewide* privatization of foster care and "related services over the course of the next few years." The legislation defines related services as family preservation, independent living, emergency shelter, residential group foster care, therapeutic foster care, intensive residential treatment, foster care supervision, case management, post-placement supervision, permanent foster care, and family reunification.

The state intends to apply for a Title IV-E waiver, which has not been approved.

District 8: Sarasota County Coalition for Families and Children

Beginning in January 1997, the state agency transferred responsibility for coordinating the care of all children in the child welfare system in the Sarasota and Fort Meyers area to the Sarasota Coalition for Families and Children. It is a lead agency model, with the YMCA functioning as the lead agency.

Population Served. The Coalition is responsible for all children who need protective services, foster care, and adoption services. Each year, the Coalition serves approximately 400 children.

Services. All services following investigation, IV-E eligibility, and legal activities remain the responsibility of the public agency.

Roles and Responsibilities. One Coalition member, the YMCA, is the lead agency. The YMCA is responsible for network formation and contract management with agencies in the coalition, claims approval and payment, quality assurance for the Coalition, reporting to the state agency, and delivering some services. Case management functions have been delegated to two other Coalition members.

Financial Arrangement. The lead agency receives a capitated rate of just over $4 million over a 18-month period for providing all the child welfare services needed by children in the child welfare system in the county. The Coalition bears risk for providing all the services needed—there is no protection for increased utilization.

District 13: Bridges Program (Lake and Sumter Counties)

Beginning in 1997, the contractor, Lake County Boys Ranch, began serving children in Lake County. Sumter County was phased in later that year.

Population Served. All children in Lake and Sumter Counties entering foster care for the first time through the Department's shelter care system are eligible for this initiative. The contractor served approximately 90 children last year.

Services. Services include assessment, family foster care, therapeutic foster care, group care, home-based services, and adoptions.

Roles and Responsibilities. The Department retains responsibility for investigations, Title IV-E and Medicaid determination, and all legal responsibilities.

Financial Arrangement. The contractor operated under a case rate for a period of time, but the state needed better ability to predict allocation so the case rate has been dismantled for the present. The initial case rate was $15,200 per child. The contractor now receives a capitated rate (amount unknown) to cover all referred children. The contract is for 30 months with periodic renegotiation to address rates and services.

District 4: Family Services Coalition (Jacksonville Area)

The contract began in 1997. The contract is for nine months. Four residential agencies in the Jacksonville area—the Baptist Home for Children, the Boys Home Association, the Children's Home Society, and the Jacksonville Youth Sanctuary—formed the Family Services Coalition to coordinate service delivery for all dependent adolescents in the district.

Goals. Central goals include improving the quality of services and client outcomes, better matching level of care and level of need, and improving child and family functioning.

Population Served. Children in foster care aged 12-17, and youth 18 and over in independent living are eligible for this initiative. Approximately 350 children are served each year.

Services. Administrative services, assessment, case management, emergency shelter, day treatment, permanency planning with families, kinship and family foster care, wraparound services, group care, specialized and therapeutic foster care, clinical services, and respite care are included in this initiative.

Quality and Outcomes. Reports from families, providers, and schools; pre- and post-tests; and standardized assessments are used to monitor quality requirements and outcome measures in the following areas:

- System performance indicators related to program effectiveness,
- Outcomes related to child functioning,
- Outcomes related to achievement of permanency planning goals, and
- An independent evaluation of the demonstration.

Roles and Responsibilities. The state determines eligibility for Title IV-E and Medicaid, refers children to the program, and retains all legal responsibility.

The coalition assumes primary responsibility for creating medical or service necessity criteria, and case management related to permanency planning, treatment planning, and long-term care determination, ongoing utilization management, contracting with providers, creating provider networks, tracking outcomes and system performance indicators, billing and reimbursement, and gatekeeping for certain care.

Financial Arrangements. The Coalition does not currently bear financial risk. Approximately $3 million is allocated to support this pilot.

District 1: Homeward Bound (Escambia and Santa Rosa Counties)

This pilot has been underway since 1992 in the Pensacola area. The contractor is the Children's Home Society (CHS).

Population Served. Children ranging from birth to age 18, in foster care for the first time, and children previously in the program that have returned due to a placement disruption are eligible for this initiative. The program will serve approximately 150 children annually.

Services. Foster care, reunification, and family support services are included in this initiative.

Financing. No financial risk is shared with CHS. The Department makes fixed monthly payments to CHS to cover room and board and support services. Approximately $1 million is allocated to this program.

GEORGIA

MATCH (Multi-Agency Team for Children Program)

The Multi-Agency Team for Children (MATCH) Program serves all children with SED regardless of their custody status. This statewide initiative, which began in 1994, includes changes in the management and delivery of child welfare services and involves the delivery of mental health treatment to Children with SED. This includes therapeutic placements such as foster care and residential treatment. Children in kinship care are referred for MATCH, but would not receive MATCH services while in the kinship home.

The MATCH Program is administered by a collaborative of state-level child welfare, juvenile justice, children's mental health and mental retardation agencies, and the Education Department.

Goals. Central goals include allowing providers the flexibility to provide individualized and accessible care, better matching level of care and level of need, ensuring placement in the least restrictive level of care, and identifying and eliminating service gaps.

Populations Served. Children with SED regardless of custody status who are served by the child welfare and mental health systems are eligible for this initiative.

According to the 1998 GAO Report, *Child Welfare: Early Experiences Implementing a Managed Care Approach* [GAO 1998], the initiative serves 660 children who are in therapeutic residential settings. This represents 3% of the state's total child welfare population.

Services. Services include case management, treatment foster care, group care, residential care/treatment, and therapeutic wilderness camps.

Quality and Outcomes. This initiative uses utilization, cost, and performance data from MIS tracking systems to monitor outcomes and quality requirements in the following areas:

- Specific system performance indicators related to program effectiveness,
- Specific criteria related to cost,
- Specific criteria related to access/availability of services and utilization patterns,
- Consumer satisfaction requirement,
- Outcomes related to child functioning,
- Credentialing requirements for individual providers,
- Specific criteria or standards related to cultural competence of providers or managed care entities, and
- An independent evaluation of the initiative/demonstration.

Roles and Responsibilities. The MATCH collaborative will have primary responsibility for coordinating service delivery, creating service necessity criteria, pre-authorizing care, gatekeeping for certain care, ongoing utilization management, tracking outcomes and system performance indicators, case management related to treatment planning, long-term care determination, and placement services, and the collection of data for the purpose of meeting state and federal reporting requirements.

Financial Arrangements. A combination of state and federal (Title IV-E) child welfare and Medicaid dollars are contributed to this initiatives approximate annual budget of $46 million. The initiative does not involve sharing financial risk with providers.

Hawaii

The state has a performance-based reimbursement initiative underway, Ohana Family Conferencing, designed to divert at-risk children and families from involvement with the CPS system.

The state also described its innovative efforts, Family Navigators and Blueprint for Change to divert placement of low-risk cases from formal involvement with the CPS or court system.

Ohana Family Conferencing

This "court diversion" demonstration has implemented changes in the management, delivery, financing, and contracting of services.

The state and county child welfare agencies, consumers, juvenile and family court, Edna McConnell Clark Foundation, National Council of Family Court Judges, juvenile justice agency, Center for Alternative Dispute Resolution, Mediation Center of Hawaii, individuals interested in being facilitators, and a policy group consisting of representatives from the judiciary, the Department of Humans Services, and the Waianae community were involved in the planning and implementation process.

Goals. Central goals include increasing prevention efforts to better protect children "at risk," decrease out-of-home care placement, diverting low-risk CPS cases out of the formal CPS system, and decreasing the length of time CPS cases are active.

Populations Served. Children at risk of entering custody and their families are eligible for this initiative. Approximately 100 children from the Waianae region of the Leeward Coast of Oahu will receive services under the auspices of this initiative.

Services. Services include case management, children protective services intake and investigation, family preservation and support services, kinship care, family foster care, individual family counseling, outreach, sex abuse treatment, information sharing among professionals and the family, negotiations, and private family time.

Quality and Outcomes. Quality requirements and outcome measures will be monitored in the following areas:

- Specific system performance indicators related to program effectiveness,
- Consumer satisfaction requirement,
- Outcomes related to child functioning,

- Outcomes related to family functioning,
- Outcomes related to the achievement of permanency planning goal,
- Credentialing requirements for individual providers,
- Accreditation of agencies/facilities according to national standards,
- Specific criteria or standards related to cultural competence of providers or managed care entities, and
- An independent evaluation of the demonstration by the University of Hawaii.

Roles and Responsibilities. The county child welfare agency has primary responsibility for the following functions: pre-authorizing and gatekeeping for care, ongoing utilization management, creating provider networks, tracking outcomes and system performance indicators, case management, billing and reimbursement, and the collection of data for the purpose of meeting state and federal reporting requirements. The state child welfare agency has primary responsibility for contracting with providers.

Financial Arrangements. During the first year of this initiative, the Edna McConnell Clark Foundation and the National Council of Family Court Judges provided $62,450 to support this initiative. Child welfare and juvenile justice now support the initiative.

The demonstration includes risk sharing with providers through the establishment of bonuses and penalties related to outcome measurements/performance-based contracts. The state child welfare agency negotiated the contracts with the providers. The contracts do not include a mechanism for risk adjustment or limit the use/amount of potential retained savings of the providers.

ILLINOIS

Illinois is a Title IV-E waiver demonstration state. Illinois' waiver, Subsidized Guardianship, allows the state to provide subsidy payments for foster parents and kin who obtain legal guardianship and provide stable placements for children who cannot be reunited or adopted. Average payments range from $343 to $415 per month and are based on the amount of board payment the state was previously paying for that child. The state intends to place 8,000 children under these arrangements statewide. The major goals include providing more stable placements, reducing agency intrusion in family life, and reducing agency costs. The state will randomly assign eligible cases to control and experimental groups.

In addition to the Title IV-E waiver, the state reported two related innovative initiatives, Performance Contracting and Front End Redesign. Performance Contracting is described below.

Performance Contracting

This initiative changed the way in which relative (kinship) care and traditional foster care services are contracted and reimbursed by the state. During FY98 (July 1, 1997 through June 30, 1998) Performance Contracting included only Cook County relative caregiver cases, totaling approximately 22,000 children. Effective FY99 (July 1, 1998 through June 30, 1999) Performance Contracting was expanded to include regular foster care in Cook County and both relative and regular foster care throughout the rest of the state. In total, an estimated 35,000 children were included from Cook County and downstate contracts.

Goals. Central goals include ensuring more efficient use of limited resources, improving the quality of services and client outcomes, controlling, predicting, and limiting costs, increasing permanency in the shortest time possible, and identifying and eliminating service gaps.

Populations Served. During FY98, approximately 22,000 children in the home of a relative (kinship care) were served. The expansion to traditional foster care and populations outside of Cook County is estimated to bring the total population to 35,850 during FY99. This represents approximately 80% of the state child welfare population.

Services. Services include case management, family preservation and support services, family foster care, kinship care, adoption, and respite care.

Quality and Outcomes. Utilization, cost, and performance data from MIS tracking systems are used to monitor outcomes and quality requirements in the following areas:

- Specific system performance indicators related to program effectiveness,
- Specific criteria related to access/availability of services and utilization patterns,
- Specific criteria related to appropriateness of services,
- Outcomes related to achievement of permanency goals, and

- Accreditation of agencies according to national standards such as COA and JCAHO.

Roles and Responsibilities. The state retains primary responsibility for pre-authorizing care, contracting with providers, tracking outcomes and system performance indicators, billing and reimbursement, and case management related to permanency planning.

Financial Arrangements. Child welfare funds support the initiative. Although a Title IV-E waiver was not required to implement performance contracting, the subsidized guardianship waiver has played a crucial role in its success. During FY98, the budget for this initiative was $202 million, with $113 million for case management and $89 million for board payments. The total budget for FY 99 is $334 million, with $122 million for relative care case management, $96 million for relative care board payments, $70 million for case management for traditional foster care, and $45 million for traditional foster care board payments. This represents approximately one-fourth of the state child welfare budget.

Reimbursement to providers is linked to performance, and providers have the opportunity to benefit or lose in several ways:

- Agencies that move more than the contracted number of children into permanent living arrangements do not experience a reduction in case management payments.

- Agencies that move more than the contracted number of children into permanent living arrangements may receive up to $2,000 per permanency above the standard payment. Each placement that results in a "pay-out" will be replaced with another referral.

- An agency could lose up to 33% of its contract in one year if it does not achieve the performance standards included in the contract because it will not continue to receive referrals.

- An agency's contract may be cancelled if its uncompensated care (cases in excess of the payment level) exceeds 20% of its total caseload.

Results to Date. Performance Contracting was initially implemented in Cook County for relative foster care in July 1997. During the first year, the relative foster care caseload declined for the first time in over a decade—decreasing 15%. Performance Contracting also helped boost the adoption and guardianship rates in Cook County home of relative care from 0.5 per 100 child cases during the third quarter of FY97 to 6.2 per 100 child cases during the first quarter of FY98. In addition, instability rates were cut in half and an estimated 250 children remained in less restrictive and less costly placements. (Illinois' achievements in permanency have since been recognized nationally. In December 1998, Illinois was recognized by President Clinton for best performance nationally in meeting the Administration's *Adoption 2002* goals.)

Current data suggest to the Department that the promising trends are sustainable. As of December 1998, the Cook County relative care caseload was at 18,892. The state anticipates the July 1999 contracted caseload in Cook County relative care to be approximately 16,715. This represents a decline of 7,726 cases or 32% over a two-year period.

INDIANA

Child Welfare Demonstration Project (Title IV-E Foster Care Waiver)

Implementation of the state's Title IV-E Waiver, Intensive Home and Community-Based Services, began on January 1, 1998. The demonstration changes the management, delivery, financing, and contracting of certain services. The state and county child welfare agencies, the state Medicaid and mental health agencies, state alcohol and drug abuse agency, private providers, Department of Education, juvenile corrections, the Family and Social Service Administration/Division of Developmental Disabilities, and the juvenile and family court were involved in the planning process.

The purpose of the initiative is to "increase home-based and community-based placement alternatives by diverting per diem funds that would have been used for more restrictive placements."

Goals. Central goals include increasing the safety and well-being of children, reducing placement in out-of-state facilities, promoting permanence, improving youth and caretaker satisfaction, and decreasing out-of-home care placement.

Populations Served. Children in state custody, including those in out-of-home care, children with SED in state custody, children served by child welfare agencies who are not in state custody, and families of children in or at risk of entering state custody are eligible for this initiative. At any given time, 4,000 children will receive services under the authority of this demonstration. The estimated stay in the project is 20 months per child.

Prospective children will be identified at the local level by the Child in Need of Services (CHINS) placement process, substantiated reports of abuse and neglect, and through the placement process for adjudicated delinquent children.

It is expected that all of the state's 92 counties will agree to participate in the five-year demonstration project. Eighty-five of the 92 counties had an approved plan for participation in place as of December 23, 1998.

Services. Services include case management, family preservation and support, permanency planning with families, kinship care, family and treatment foster care, Healthy Families Indiana services (home visitations for at-risk infants in overburdened families), special education or alternative schooling, substance abuse treatment, conflict resolution and anger management, sexual abuse treatment, respite care, individual and group counseling, supportive services to caretakers, independent living services, behavior management, and psychiatric services including medication and access to crisis services.

The demonstration will provide caretaker ratios of up to one-to-one at all times and will provide team job training for juvenile probation officers, child welfare caseworkers, and other community stakeholders. At the time of entry into the system and just prior to exit, the Indiana Child Welfare Information System (ICWIS) will collect data on each child in the system to describe risk assessment demographics.

Quality and Outcomes. Quality requirements and outcomes will be monitored in the following areas:

- Cost neutrality,
- Outcomes related to child functioning (improved school performance, decreased delinquent behavior, or transitioning a child to an independent living environment),
- Outcomes related to family functioning,
- Outcomes permanency planning (timelier adoptions), and
- The Institute for Applied Research will conduct an independent evaluation of the initiative.

Roles and Responsibilities. The state child welfare agency, through its county child welfare offices, shares responsibility with juvenile and family courts (courts that evaluate and reexamine child welfare protocols regularly) and other local agencies for the following functions: determination of Title IV-E eligibility, creating service necessity criteria, ongoing utilization management, contracting with providers, tracking outcomes and system performance indicators, case management, and the collection of data for the purpose of meeting state and federal reporting requirements. The county child welfare agency assumes primary responsibility for pre-authorizing and gatekeeping for care.

Service coordination at the local level is the responsibility of an interagency agreement between child welfare, juvenile court judges, mental health, education, and the Step Ahead Council.

Financial Arrangements. Child welfare, mental health, Medicaid, education, and juvenile justice are contributing funds to this initiative. A case rate of no more than $9,000 in flexible funding will be available for each child chosen for participation in this initiative. The federal/state and county shares are expected to remain at approximately the same level as prior to the implementation of the initiative (61% and 39% respectively) of that total.

The first 24 months of the Project has a budget of $20.4 million. The Title IV-E waiver creates funding flexibility necessary to support this initiative. The full value of the flexible funding is $36 million annually, with funding saved or cost averted anticipated in the 20th month. The savings will be reinvested in the project.

KANSAS

Statewide Privatization Initiatives for Adoption, Family Preservation, and Foster Care

Kansas has privatized all child welfare services with the exception of CPS intake and investigations. The Governor's Office, state legislature, child welfare agency, Medicaid agency, mental health agency, alcohol and drug abuse agency, nonprofit private providers, consumers and the juvenile and family court were involved in the planning process that preceded the statewide implementation that was completed in 1997.

More recently, in September 1998, the state was granted a Title IV-E waiver to test different payment systems (fixed case rates vs. fee-for-service) to enable private providers to offer enhanced services to families.

Goals. Central goals include improving client outcomes, increasing permanency in the shortest time possible, increasing prevention efforts to better protect children "at risk," and decategorizing or "pooling funding" to create a more seamless system of care.

Populations Served. All children in state custody, including those in out-of-home care, children in out-of-county or out-of-state placements, adoptive families and children with adoption as the permanency goal, children with SED in state custody, and families of children in state custody or at risk of entering custody are eligible for this initiative.

During the past year 2,422 families received family preservation services, 1,404 children received adoption services, and 5,693 children received foster care services.

The state projects that during the upcoming year 2,472 families will receive family preservation services, 1,053 children will receive adoption services, and 4,430 children will receive foster care services.

Services provided under the adoption, family preservation, and foster care contracts. Services include case management, emergency shelter, family preservation and support services, day treatment, permanency planning with families, kinship care, family foster care, treatment foster care, group care, residential care/treatment, psychiatric hospitalization, adoption recruitment and services, mental health services for children and families, independent living, respite care, and wraparound services.

Quality and Outcomes. Reports from providers and utilization, cost, and performance data from an MIS tracking system are used to monitor quality requirements and outcomes in the following areas:

- Specific system performance indicators related to program effectiveness (children will be safe from abuse and or neglect, children shall remain in the same foster care placement pending adoption),

- Specific criteria related to access/availability of services and utilization patterns (contractor shall accept all referrals),

- Consumer satisfaction (siblings should be kept together, adoptive family members shall be satisfied with adoptive services, families receiving preservation services will be satisfied with the services provided),

- Outcomes related to achievement of permanency planning goals (children are reunited with their families in a timely manner, children whose permanency plan is adoption will be placed in a timely manner),

- Outcomes related to recidivism/reentry (children from families receiving family preservation services will not require out-of-home placement, adjudicated juvenile offenders will not re-offend, foster children reunited with families will not reenter the system),

- Requirements to adhere to professional standards or licensing requirements,
- Credentialing requirements for individual providers,
- Accreditation of agencies/facilities according to national standards,
- Specific criteria or standards related to cultural competence of providers or managed care entities (children maintain family, community, and cultural ties, children experience a minimal number of moves while in care, and
- An independent evaluation of the initiative.

Roles and Responsibilities. The state child welfare agency has retained primary responsibility for the following functions: determining Title IV-E or Medicaid eligibility, pre-authorizing and gatekeeping for certain care, child protective services intake, oversight of ongoing utilization management, contracting with nonprofit lead agencies that function as managed care entities, tracking outcomes and system performance indicators, case management related to permanency planning, billing and reimbursement, and collecting data for the purpose of meeting state and federal reporting requirements.

Not-for-profit lead agencies have assumed primary responsibility for the following functions: creating medical necessity and service necessity criteria, contracting with providers and creating provider networks, and case management related to treatment planning, long-term care determination, placement services, and behavioral health services.

Financial Arrangements. During the past year, $86,400,000 was spent on the privatization initiatives. The projected budget for the upcoming year is $102 million. This initiative represents 56% of child welfare spending in Kansas.

The state is currently sharing risk with providers. Providers receive the following case rates for delivery of the following services:

Type of Service	Case Rate	Population	Length of Time
Family Preservation	$3,719	Family	12 months
Foster Care	$14,022	Child	12 months, postpermanency
Adoption	$14,746	Child	18 months, postfinalization

The case rates that are listed above are "episodic" case rates. "Episodic" case rates require the lead agencies to be responsible for all costs of care and treatment for the child and family from the time that the agency receives the case until 12-18 months after the child has been reunified with his/her family, or entered an alternative permanent placement. The rates were established during the contract negotiation based on the rates that providers bid to the state. The initiative does not impose any limits on potential profits or retained savings of the providers. However, the state did include a risk adjustment mechanism for providers during the first year, which required providers to be responsible for the first 10% of expenditures over the allocated budget and the state was responsible for the remaining expenditures.

Following the completion of the first year of the initiative it was apparent that the risk-sharing corridor, as defined in the initial contract, was inadequate for the needs of the lead foster care agencies. During contract renewal, the state made the following case rate adjustments: the foster care case rate was increased by $1,500 per case for all year two referrals and each lead agency was allowed to assign 150 children per year to a system of traditional fee-for-service reimbursement outside of the initiative's case rate. Additionally, an amendment was added that provides lead agencies with a one-time lump sum payment of $28,500 payment to each lead agencies for all transfer cases (children and families already in the system at the time the statewide privatization took effect) who were still in the system on July 1, 1998.

Kentucky

Quality Care Pilot

The state plans to change how services are managed, financed, and contracted for 100 children and families in this pilot project. The state legislature, state child welfare agency, and nonprofit private providers were involved in the planning process.

Goals. Central goals include decreasing length of stay in out-of-home care, improving client outcomes, improving the quality of services, and providing individualized and accessible care.

Population Served. Children in certain out-of-home care arrangements and their families are eligible for this initiative. This pilot will serve approximately 100 children and their families residing in (or receiving services in) the Jefferson, Bluegrass, Northern Kentucky, or Green River regions.

Services. Services include case management, permanency planning with families, treatment foster care, residential care/treatment, adoption services, and wraparound services.

Quality and Outcomes. Reports from families and providers, an internal review conducted by selected staff, and independent review by the Children's Review Program will be used to monitor quality requirements and outcomes in the following areas:

- System performance indicators related to program effectiveness (children are safe from maltreatment),
- Criteria related to cost (case rates paid in installments depend upon the success of the child's placement at/and past discharge),
- Development of Level of Care criteria or clinical protocols (that the enrolled child will have a valid level assigned by the Children's Review Program prior to admission),
- Consumer satisfaction requirement that clients will be satisfied with services (a client satisfaction survey upon case closure will measure the number and percent of parents and youth reporting satisfaction with services),
- Outcomes related to child functioning (maintaining reunification or permanency goal for six months, success includes extended interruptions from AWOL),
- Outcomes related to family functioning (maintaining reunification or permanency goal for six months),
- Outcomes related to the achievement of permanency planning goals (children are reunited with their families in a timely manner according to their permanency plan),
- Outcomes related to placement stability (children experience a minimum number of placements),
- Requirements to adhere to professional standards or licensing requirements (subcontractors/providers must be able to meet applicable JCAHO or COA standards), and
- Criteria or standards related to cultural competence of providers or managed care entities (children maintain family, community, and cultural ties).

Roles and Responsibilities. The state child welfare agency will retain primary responsibility for contracting with providers tracking outcomes and system performance indicators, and billing and reimbursement.

Initially, under a no-risk contract, a not-for-profit lead agency will assume primary responsibility for gatekeeping for certain care, ongoing utilization management, case management, and data collection to meet state and federal reporting requirements.

Financial Arrangements. The allocated budget for FY99 is $3 million, all of which will be drawn from state child welfare funds. No regulatory or legislative changes have been necessary thus far, and the initiative does not involve a Medicaid or Title IV-E waiver. However, the state will need to file for a regulation waiver for the pilot to implement the contract for services that are different from the current system of child welfare operation.

The state child welfare agency plans to negotiate a contract to share financial risk with service providers within the year. The contracts will include a case rate based on the level of care assigned to a child at the time of intake. The contract will not contain a risk adjustment mechanism or limit the use of potential retained savings for providers, but will transfer increasing responsibility for service provision to the child's family to the provider.

Maryland

Maryland has been granted a Title IV-E waiver to support an Assisted Guardianship demonstration. The state will provide subsidy payments and services to foster parents and kin that receive AFDC/TANF child-only payments if they obtain legal guardianship of the child. Payments will be $300 per month. Children must be in stable placements and have adoption and reunification ruled out as permanency options. The state reported another initiative in the child welfare arena.

Baltimore City Child Welfare Managed Care Pilot

This citywide demonstration will change how services are managed, delivered, financed, and contracted. The initiative will serve approximately 20% of the paid foster care population in the city.

Broad input was sought during the planning process. Local and state agencies drafted the RFP, and Baltimore City Department of Social Services issued it. The proposal has been awarded but the final contract has not been signed. The initiative is scheduled for implementation within the year.

Goals. Central goals include decreasing the length of stay in out-of-home care, reducing the rate of reentry into care, reduction of congregate care for children ages 0-5, and increasing permanency in the shortest time possible.

Populations Served. Eligible populations include children in paid out-of-home care in the following target groups: children ages 0-5, children who have recently entered care, children in kinship care recently converted to kinship foster care, and the siblings and families of eligible children. 1,000 children and their families will be served.

Services. Services include case management, emergency shelter, permanency planning with families, kinship care (licensed as foster parents), family foster care, treatment foster care, group care, residential care/treatment, adoption recruitment and services, wraparound services, respite care, independent living, and birth parent services.

Quality and Outcomes. The courts and the foster care review board will continue to provide oversight. Reports from families, providers, and schools; standardized assessments (Child Well-Being Scale); utilization, cost, and performance data from MIS tracking systems; case record reviews; case plan changes; court report approval; abuse and neglect tracking; unusual incident reports; and client complaints and appeals will be used to monitor quality requirements and outcomes in the following areas:

- System performance indicators related to program effectiveness:
  - reduction in the length of time a child age 5 or less is in placement (816 care days in three years),
  - reduction in care days for children entering care at the time of disposition by the court (755 care days in three years),
  - reduction in care days for children converting from kinship to foster care or children not otherwise in a target group who are siblings of project children (879 care days), and
  - reduction in the number of care days spent in congregate care by children age 0-5 (133 care days in three years).
- Criteria related to cost (must be cost neutral),
- Development of level of care criteria or clinical protocols),
- Consumer satisfaction, based on client complaints and appeals),
- Outcomes related to child functioning, based on the Child Well-Being Scales,
- Outcomes related to achievement of permanency planning goals (an increase in the number of children for whom a permanency plan is achieved [316 out of 1,000]),
- Outcomes related to recidivism/reentry (decrease in the number of unplanned reentries into care [84 out of 1,000]),
- Requirements to adhere to professional standards or licensing requirements (primary contractor and all child placement subcontractors must be licensed child placement agencies),

- Specific criteria or standards related to cultural competence of providers or managed care entities on which proposals are rated, and
- An independent evaluation of the initiative.

Roles and Responsibilities. The Baltimore City child welfare agency will retain primary responsibility for determining Title IV-E or Medicaid eligibility, contracting with a private child welfare managed care entity, tracking outcomes and system performance indicators, billing and reimbursement, and collecting data to meet state and federal reporting requirements. The public agency is also responsible for determining whether the lead agency can access the financial stop loss provision.

A nonprofit lead agency, which is under a three-year risk-shared contract, will be required to assume responsibility for case management services, ongoing utilization management, creating provider networks, and providing a full range of placement and support services for enrolled children and their families for the duration of the contract. The vendor is responsible for the provision of services for three years regardless of whether children and families exit and reenter care.

Financial Arrangements. The budget for this initiative will be provided by child welfare funds. Project children are also eligible for Medical Assistance. Vendors are encouraged to access Medical Assistance along with other community resources, to supplement the case rate.

The city child welfare administration plans to share financial risk with the lead agency by contracting a case rate for a three-year period, however, this rate has not yet been established. A competitive bidding process determined the case rate ceiling. The risk-share arrangement includes a stop-loss provision to adjust risk. If the contractor places a child in a setting that costs more than $3,500 per month, it must pay the entire cost or apply for approval from the Baltimore City Department of Social Services. Any potential savings or profits from the project must be reinvested in services for children and families involved in the project. The initiative does not plan to share risk with a for-profit MCO. For-profit MCOs may be subcontracted by the lead agency, but they can not provide child placement services. The state plans to apply for a new Title IV-E waiver that will provide funding flexibility for this initiative, if approved. However, the state will proceed without the waiver, if its application is denied.

MASSACHUSETTS

The state reported two initiatives: 1) Massachusetts Commonworks, which began implementation in June 1996 and provides foster care and residential care to approximately 1,000 children and youth annually, and 2) the Family-Based Services Initiative, which will be implemented within a year.

Massachusetts Commonworks

Massachusetts Commonworks is a statewide initiative. Nonprofit private providers and the state child welfare agency were involved in planning the initiative. The state released both a Request for Information (RFI) and an RFP before selecting the six lead agencies and the ASO. Implementation is now complete. The financing arrangements for the lead agencies recently changed from no-risk to case rates.

Goals. Central goals include decreasing the length of stay in out-of-home care, ensuring placement in the least restrictive level of care, increasing permanency in the shortest time possible, and improving family and child functioning.

Populations Served. Commonworks serves adolescents in state custody requiring group or residential care. The lead agencies have managed the care of 950 children and their families during the past year and the state agency projects that the initiative will provide services to 1,100 children and families during the next fiscal year.

Services. Services include case management, family preservation and support services, treatment foster care, group care, residential care/treatment, substance abuse services for children and adolescents, wraparound services, and independent living services.

Quality and Outcomes. Reports from providers and schools, site visits, records reviews, and utilization, cost, and performance data from MIS tracking systems will be used to monitor quality requirements and outcomes in the following areas:

- System performance indicators related to program effectiveness (clients' overall progress in treatment, timely achievement of treatment plan goals, and reduced lengths of stay),
- Criteria related to cost (cost of services within Commonworks and cost of education services for Commonworks clients),
- Criteria related to access/availability of services and utilization, including

- placement utilization into programs operated directly by the lead agency,
- timely and accurate maintenance of service authorizations,
- submission of accurate and timely claims,
- timely and accurate maintenance of provider files,
- timely completion of initial referral plans, treatment plan summaries, treatment progress reviews and discharge plans, and
- timely reporting of critical incidents.
- Criteria related to appropriateness of services,
- Development of Level of Care criteria or clinical protocols,
- Consumer satisfaction requirement (children will complete satisfaction surveys),
- Family participation will be monitored,
- Outcomes related to child functioning (improvement in areas defined in treatment planning),
- Outcomes related to family functioning (improvement in areas defined in treatment planning),
- Outcomes related to achievement of permanency planning goals,
- Credentialing requirements for individuals providers, and
- An independent evaluation of the initiative/demonstration.

Roles and Responsibilities. The state child welfare agency retains primary responsibility for the following functions: determining Title IV-E or Medicaid eligibility, approving medical necessity or service necessity criteria, pre-authorizing initial care and referral to lead agencies, contract management with lead agencies and the ASO that provides administrative support services, and case management specifically related to permanency planning.

Under the no-risk ASO contract, OPTIONS/Commonworks, a for-profit behavioral health managed care organization, has primary responsibility for monitoring and reporting the use of services; implementing and monitoring quality evaluations and system improvements; developing and implementing an information system; developing the financial reporting system; developing and implementing the billing and payment system; tracking grievances and complaints; reviewing, monitoring, and reporting on the credentialing of all direct service providers; tracking outcomes and system performance indicators; and collecting data to meet state and federal reporting requirements.

Meanwhile, a risk-share contract established that the lead not-for-profit provider agencies are responsible for service authorization and care coordination, ongoing utilization management and clinical review, creating provider networks and contract management with providers, fee negotiation/claims approval, and case management related to treatment planning, long-term care determination, placement services, and services for mental health or substance abuse treatment for families.

Financial Arrangements. The state child welfare agency entirely funds this initiative. It allocated $38 million last year, and $45 million for the next fiscal year. The agency expects the budget for the fully implemented initiative to represent approximately 11% of the total child welfare budget. The state is considering applying for a Title IV-E waiver for aftercare services, potentially altering the financing arrangement and demanding regulatory changes.

The risk-share contract with the lead agencies establishes a per-child/per-month case rate of $4,447 to provide any and all services covered under the initiative until the case is closed. The state child welfare administration negotiated the contract with providers by evaluating the actual costs that were paid during the first year of the initiative under a no-risk contract and incorporating inflation and projections of length of stay. Providers are protected by an arrangement that shares risk at the following rates: 1% shared risk for the first four months, 2% shared risk for the second four months, and 3% shared risk for the final four months of the contract year. The contract also includes a requirement that potential profits of lead agencies are limited to 5% of the budget.

The state is paying the managed care entity $2.2 million on a fee-for-service arrangement for the provision of administrative and management support services, representing about 6% of the total budget.

Massachusetts's Family-Based Services Initiative

This statewide initiative is a result of a collaborative planning process between the state child welfare agency and the state Medicaid agency, and will begin implementing changes in the way services are managed, delivered, financed, and contracted within one year.

Goals. Central goals include providing individualized and accessible care, providing more appropriate levels of care, decategorizing or "pooling funding" to create a more seamless system of care, increasing wraparound services, and improving coordination of services.

Populations Served. Eligible populations include children in out-of-home foster care arrangements, adoptive families and children with adoption as the permanency goal, children with SED in state custody, families of children in state custody, and families of children at risk of entering custody.

Services. Services will include emergency shelter, family preservation and support services, day treatment, mental health and substance abuse treatment for children and families, wraparound services, and respite care.

Quality and Outcomes. Reports from families, providers, and schools; standardized assessments; and utilization, cost, and performance data from MIS tracking systems will be used to monitor quality requirements and outcomes in the following areas:

- Specific system performance indicators related to program effectiveness,
- Specific criteria related to access/availability of services and utilization patterns,
- Outcomes related to child and family functioning,
- Outcomes related to achievement of permanency planning goals,
- Requirements to adhere to professional standards or licensing requirements,
- Credentialing requirements for individual providers,
- Specific criteria or standards related to cultural competence of providers or managed care entities, and
- An independent evaluation of the initiative.

Roles and Responsibilities. The state child welfare agency will retain primary responsibility for pre-authorizing care, collecting data to meet state and federal reporting requirements, and case management related to permanency planning, treatment planning, long-term care determination, and monitoring placement services.

Under a no-risk share contract, a not-for-profit lead agency/provider will assume primary responsibility for creating medical necessity or service necessity criteria, gatekeeping for certain care, ongoing utilization management, creating networks and contracting with providers, tracking outcomes and system performance indicators, and fee negotiations and claims payment.

Financial Arrangements. The state child welfare agency will contribute 100% of the $31 million budget allocated for the upcoming fiscal year.

MICHIGAN

Michigan's Families

This Title IV-E waiver demonstration project plans to implement changes in the management, delivery, financing, and contracting of services during the next year for eligible populations from six pilot sites by utilizing the funding flexibility available through the federal Title IV-E waiver the state has been awarded. The state and local child welfare agencies, state Medicaid office, local community mental health boards, Department of Education, nonprofit private providers, juvenile and family courts, and local interagency collaboratives were involved in planning the wraparound initiative. These stakeholders were chosen to ensure that the demonstration was locally determined.

Goals. Central goals include decreasing the length of stay in out-of-home care, decategorizing or "pooling funding" to create a more seamless system of care, decreasing out-of-home care placement, and developing community-based, collaborative wraparound models.

Populations Served. Populations eligible for this initiative include all children in state custody in out-of-home care, children with SED in custody, children with SED not in custody, children served by child welfare agencies who are not in custody, families of children in state custody or at risk of entry into custody, and children involved with the juvenile justice system.

Minimally, 120 children and families will participate in this demonstration. Each site must have the capacity to serve a minimum of 20 Title IV-E eligible children at any time. Sites could elect to include *all* Title IV-E eligible children and any other "community kids" with SED needs who can be supported by funds other than Title IV-E.

Services. Using a wraparound philosophy of care, the initiative may include the delivery of case management, family preservation and support services, day treatment, permanency planning with families, kinship care, family foster care, treatment foster care, group care, residential care/treatment, psychiatric hospitalization, juvenile justice, mental health and substance abuse treatment, and respite care.

Quality and Outcomes. Reports from families, providers, and schools; standardized assessments; pre- and post-test; and utilization, cost, and performance data from MIS tracking systems will be used by the state of Michigan to monitor outcomes and quality requirements in the following areas:

- System performance indicators related to program effectiveness (ensuring safety and increasing availability and quality of services),
- Criteria related to cost (cost neutrality and the extent that the demonstration results in a shift in expenditures from out-of-home placements to in-home and preventive services),
- Criteria related to access/availability of services and utilization patterns (assuring more timely access to services, and increasing the levels and types of services),
- Consumer satisfaction requirement,
- Outcomes related to child functioning (determine whether the well-being of children and families increased or diminished under the demonstration project using the Child and Adolescent Functional Assessment Scale),
- Outcomes related to family functioning (determine whether the well-being of children and families increased or diminished under the demonstration project),
- Outcomes related to achievement of permanency planning goals (to expedite permanency, measure the permanence and level of restrictiveness, reduce length of time in out-of-home placement, and decrease out-of-home placements),
- Outcomes related to recidivism/reentry (reduce reentry rates),
- An independent evaluation of the initiative/demonstration, and
- Evaluation of organizational and service aspects.

The state will also examine the differences in outcome measures listed above by controlling for such variables as age, race and/or gender and the potential impact of contextual factors. The RFP calls for the bidders to describe their approach to outcome management. The state does require that each of the proposals include specific criteria related to cost neutrality, a consumer satisfaction requirement, outcomes related to child and family functioning, and an independent evaluation of the demonstration.

Roles and Responsibilities. The state child welfare agency will retain primary responsibility for contracting with a lead contractor in each selected site, tracking outcomes and system performance indicators, collecting data to meet state and federal reporting requirements, and determining Title IV-E eligibility.

The state will enter into a risk-share contract with the lead contractor in each local collaborative. The lead contractor is responsible for the following functions: creation of medical necessity or service necessity criteria, pre-authorizing and gatekeeping for care, ongoing utilization management, contracting with providers, creating provider networks, case management, fee negotiation, claims approval and reimbursement, and financial risk management.

Financial Arrangements. The state will pay the contractor a case rate of $1,500 per month per enrolled Title IV-E child. The contractor will negotiate the rates for providers. The sites have the option to include only Title IV-E eligible children and families or designate some non-Title IV-E eligible children and families as eligible for service. Non-Title IV-E children will be supported by pooled or shared funds from multiple state or local agencies. The goal is to maximize state and local resources to supplement the Title IV-E case rate and to enhance services for both Title IV-E and non-Title IV-E children and families who are enrolled.

It is anticipated that selected local sites will pool or share Medicaid, child welfare, mental health, education, and/or substance abuse, and other local funds. A 10% risk corridor is included to protect the financial stability of the local collaborative and the lead agency.

Permanency-Focused Reimbursement System Pilot

In May 1997, the Michigan Family Independence Agency contracted with four providers (Catholic Social Services of Wayne County, Homes for Black Children, Orchard's Children's Services, and Spectrum Human Service), who combined to operate seven foster care programs designed to focus on outcomes instead of volume.

Goals. The central goal of the initiative is the achievement of a permanency plan for each child that includes a return to the family, placement with a relative or legal guardian, adoption, or independent living.

Populations Served. Eligible populations include children in state custody, children in state custody in out-of-home care, and families of children in custody. Approximately 650 children were served during the first year. Children ages 12 and younger, at the point of the referral, and siblings 13 years of age or older that have been assessed within the Wayne County Shelter System as appropriate for family foster care are eligible. Children who were in placement prior to the implementation of the initiative are also eligible for the services included in this initiative.

Services. The initiative includes the provision of family-focused/child-centered foster care and placement services. According to a draft study from the Center for Health Policy Research at the George Washington University Medical Center [Wehr et al. 1998], "The Contractor shall be responsible for assessing and responding to identified services needs." For parents, these may include, but not be limited to the following: homemaker, budgeting, parenting skills, safe child behavior management techniques, substance abuse services, problem-solving skills development, anger management, job preparation, life skills development, counseling, and domestic violence. Services to children, depending on their developmental stage and level of functioning, may include, but not be limited to teaching peaceful/safe problem solving, life skills development, academic tutoring, self projection techniques.

Quality and Outcomes. Quality requirements and outcome measures will be monitored in the following areas:

- Specific system performance indicators related to program effectiveness,
- Specific performance indicators related to cost,
- Specific criteria related to access/availability of services and utilization patterns,
- Specific criteria related to appropriateness of services,
- Outcomes related to child functioning,
- Outcomes related to achievement of permanency planning goals, and
- Requirements to adhere to professional standards or licensing requirements.

A successful placement is defined as a return to the child's own home, placement in a home with a relative or legal guardian, or independent living.

Roles and Responsibilities. The state child welfare agency retains primary responsibility for all management functions. According to the study from the Center for Health Policy Research alluded to earlier,

> The Contractor shall assume family responsibility in cases where any sibling is placed by the Agency in residential care under the jurisdictional authority of the neglect statute (with certain exceptions) ...Family responsibility is defined as coordinating service planning with all agencies providing placement services to the

family. Coordination means maintaining at a minimum monthly contact with other treatment and care managers as well as the family specified in the Agency's SM and insuring parental involvement in plan, permanency planning, visitations, release planning.

The not-for-profit lead agency will not reject or eject any appropriate referrals.

Financial Arrangements. Contractors are paid an initial lump-sum payment of approximately $1,770 for each eligible youth referred. Contractors will receive an additional $14.94 per day for each child referred. An additional lump sum payment of $1,500 is made for each eligible youth if either of the following are true: parental rights have been terminated within 600 days (Wayne County) or 420 days (out-of-state) from the acceptance date, or a successful placement had been made within 315 days (Wayne County) or 265 days (out-of-state) from the acceptance date. Finally, a provider receives a single lump-sum payment of $730 for each youth who sustains a successful placement for at least six consecutive months, or is placed for adoption within six months of termination of parental rights.

Youth who return to the foster care system within one year from the date of a "successful placement" are not eligible for a delayed payment, but are eligible for an initial payment and the per diem rate.

Adoption Contracting

The Michigan Family Independence Agency (FIA) implemented a contract change in 1992 to link the reimbursement of licensed private adoption agencies to the timeliness of placements.

Goals. Increasing permanency through adoption in the shortest time possible while maintaining children in their communities is the central goal of this initiative.

Populations Served. Children who are in state custody with adoption as the permanency plan are eligible for inclusion in this initiative.

Services. Services include case management, adoption recruitment, adoption services, and court related support. Contract agencies are also required to list a child on the adoption exchange if no adoptive family is identified within 90 days of permanent wardship with the plan of adoption.

Quality and Outcomes. Reports from providers and utilization, cost, and performance data from MIS tracking systems are used to monitored quality requirements and outcomes in the following areas:

- Specific system performance indicators related to program effectiveness,
- Outcomes related to child functioning,
- Outcomes related to family functioning,
- Outcomes related to achievement of permanency planning goals (40% of children placed in adoption under the supervision of the contractor for foster care services whose plan is adoption, shall be placed with an adoptive family within six months of commitment to FIA, 70% of children placed in adoption under the supervision of the contractor for foster care services whose plan is adoption, shall be placed under an adoptive family within 12 months of commitment to FIA, and 65% of children placed in adoption under supervision of the contractor for foster care services, whose plan is adoption shall be placed with at least one sibling), and
- Agencies must be licensed by the state of Michigan.

Roles and Responsibilities. The state child welfare agency retains responsibility for the determination of Title IV-E or Medicaid eligibility.

Not-for-profit providers under a risk-share contract assume primary responsibility for case management related to permanency planning, treatment planning, long-term care determination, and placement services, and data collection for the purpose of meeting state and federal reporting requirements.

Financial Arrangements. The initiative links reimbursement to the achievement of permanency.

Within six weeks of a contractor placing a child in an adoptive home, the contractor will submit a completed FIA invoice and attach the necessary documentation to obtain payment for services. Once the adoption is finalized, the contractor will submit billing documentation to receive payment for the adoption finalization. FIA shall reimburse the agency based on the established payment schedules that include differential payment for placement and finalization.

MINNESOTA

Minnesota is a county-administered state, but the Minnesota legislature created Children's Mental Health (CMH) Collaboratives. A CMH Collaborative is an entity formed by the agreement of representatives of the local system of care for the purpose of developing and governing an integrated service delivery system. CMH collaboratives bring together counties, school districts, local mental health providers, parents, corrections, public health, and other community-based organizations to meet the needs of children with SED, emotional behavioral disorders (EBD), and children at risk of these conditions. Collaboratives pool their funds and coordinate multiple services with the purpose of instituting system change through the development of an integrated service system that will meet the needs of children involved with multiple systems to expand services, decategorize them and improve their efficiency.

Hennepin County, encompassing the city of Minneapolis, was also surveyed, and reported the details of their implementation of the Children's Mental Health Collaborative. The Hennepin County Children's Mental Health Collaborative is participating in a pilot project with the state Department of Human Services, to become a prepaid provider of medical assistance services and to be eligible to receive medical assistance reimbursement.

Children's Mental Health Collaborative: Hennepin County

This countywide initiative is implementing changes in the way services are managed, financed, and contracted to the target population. The state and county child welfare agency, state Medicaid office, state mental health agency, Department of Education, nonprofit private providers, county corrections, and consumers were involved in planning the initiative.

Goals. Central goals include achieving greater system effectiveness, improving system coordination, and increasing service capacity for youth with SED and their families.

Populations Served. Youth with SED, regardless of whether they are in custody, are eligible for inclusion in this initiative. In the past year, 400 children and 300 families were provided these services. The county projects 800 children and 600 families will receive services in the next year.

Services. Services include case management, service coordination, family preservation and support services, day treatment, treatment foster care, residential care/treatment, psychiatric hospitalization, juvenile justice, mental health care for children and their families, wraparound services, respite care, and independent living services to meet the individualized needs of the family.

Quality and Outcomes. Reports from families, providers, and schools; standardized assessments; and utilization, cost, and performance data from MIS tracking systems will be used to monitor outcomes and quality requirements in the following areas:

- System performance indicators related to program effectiveness (increased child and family functioning, increased school success, and increased family satisfaction),
- Criteria related to cost (rates not to exceed Medicaid rates, and cost neutrality),
- Criteria related to appropriateness of services (decreased out-of-home placements or discharge to a less restrictive setting),
- Consumer satisfaction requirement (increased family/foster family satisfaction),
- Outcomes related to child functioning (increased school success and attendance, increased child functioning at school and in the community, decreased violent behavior, decreased out-of-home placement, and decreased placement in restrictive settings),
- Outcomes related to family functioning (improve overall family functioning in all areas of life and improve parental skills),
- Outcomes related to achievement of permanency planning goals (decreased length of stay in out-of-home placement),
- Outcomes related to recidivism/reentry (placement stabilization and decreased placement disruption),
- Requirements to adhere to professional standards or licensing requirements, and
- Specific criteria or standards related to cultural competence of providers or managed care entities.

Roles and Responsibilities. The local collaborative in Hennepin County has primary responsibility for pre-authorizing care, utilization management, provider contracting, and billing and reimbursement. The state child welfare agency and the local collaborative share responsibility for data collection and tracking.

There is some coordination between this initiative and managed health care reform for physical and behavioral health services in the county. In the next one to two years, the delivery and management of services to children with SED will become more fully integrated.

Financial Arrangements. Children's Mental Health Collaboratives pool state, local, and private funds to create "integrated funds." Local service decisionmakers can draw funding from a single local source so funds follow clients through the service delivery system.

The past year's budget was $5 million. The projected budget for the upcoming year is $7 million. Next year's funding involves a Medicaid waiver and draws funds from the state/county mental health agencies through state and federal grants and in-kind services from the county ($5 million) and the state Medicaid budget ($2 million). Sharing financial risk with a managed care organization (MCO) is under consideration.

The implementation of the initiative required that the state amend the "Minnesota Comprehensive Children's Mental Health Act" to expand the billable Medicaid services and enabling the creation of a prepaid medical assistance (managed care model).

MISSOURI

Missouri's Interdepartmental Initiative for Children with Severe Needs

This initiative changes the management, delivery, financing, and contracting of services for a select group of children with therapeutic needs.

The Governor's Office, state Medicaid agency, nonprofit private providers, consumers, child welfare, juvenile justice, psychiatric services, alcohol and drug abuse, developmental disabilities agencies, special education, and health departments were involved in planning the initiative.

The State of Missouri released an RFP for a Care Management Organization (CMO) and an RFP for a Technical Support Organization (TSO). The CMO contract was awarded to the Missouri Alliance and the TSO contract was awarded to ValueOptions. Implementation was scheduled for March 1, 1999.

Goals. Central goals include improving outcomes for children and families, providing individualized and accessible care, decategorizing or "pooling funding" from a number of state agencies to create a more seamless system of care, and maintaining children in their communities.

Populations Served. Children with SED needs from two geographic areas of the state are eligible for this initiative. It is important to note that the demonstration is not the privatization of child welfare services, but an attempt to address the behavioral health needs of children with severe needs who are served by multiple state agencies. Children in the eastern and central portions of the state (from public child welfare, juvenile justice, psychiatric services, alcohol and drug, developmental disabilities, special education, and health) are targeted for enrollment in the demonstration.

The initiative should serve up to 1,500 children and their families during the upcoming three years.

Services. Services include case management, emergency shelter, family preservation and support services, day treatment, permanency planning with families, kinship care, family foster care, treatment foster care, group care, residential care/treatment, psychiatric hospitalization, adoption recruitment and services, mental health and substance abuse treatment, juvenile justice, wraparound services, respite care, and independent living services based upon individual child and family need.

Quality and Outcomes. Reports from families, providers, and schools; standardized assessments; pre- and post-tests; interviews with stakeholders; and utilization, cost, and performance data contained in a MIS tracking system will be used to monitor outcomes and quality requirements in the following areas:

- System performance indicators related to program effectiveness (to decrease preventable hospitalizations),

- Criteria related to access/availability of services and utilization patterns (to increase Healthy Children and Youth Early Periodic Screening, Diagnosis and Treatment [EPSDT] exams for enrolled children, and to increase the incidence of physical and dental exams and treatment for enrolled children),

- Consumer satisfaction requirement (the self-report on quality of life will improve, and the Care Management Organization will provide mechanisms for identifying and monitoring outcomes and system performance indicators that address child and family participation and satisfaction),

- Outcomes related to child functioning:
  - percentage of enrolled children who obtain high school diploma/GED will increase,
  - percentage of enrolled children who drop out, are suspended, or expelled from school will be reduced,
  - employment of enrolled children over age 16 that are not attending school will increase,
  - percentage of enrolled children who participate in community activities will increase,

- functionality on standardized measures will improve for enrolled children,
- incidence of sexually transmitted diseases (STDs) and pregnancy among enrolled children will decrease,
- incidence of substance abuse among enrolled children will decrease,
- percentage of enrolled children who attempt suicide and commit crimes against persons will be reduced, and
- percentage of enrolled children who are involved in noncriminal aggression, on runaway status, and who are adjudicated will be reduced.

• Outcomes related to family functioning (the percentage of enrolled children under court custody will decrease, placement disruptions for enrolled children will decrease, and the incidence of crime and substance abuse among enrolled parents will decrease),

• Outcomes related to achievement of permanency planning goals (the percentage of children in a permanent family will increase),

• Outcomes related to recidivism/reentry (the percentage of enrolled children who are repeat victims of abuse and neglect will be reduced and the percentage of enrolled family members who are involved in repeat abuse and neglect will be reduced),

• Credentialing requirements for individual providers and accreditation of agencies/facilities according to national standards,

• Specific criteria or standards related to cultural competence of providers, and

• An independent evaluation of the initiative/demonstration.

Roles and Responsibilities. A multidepartmental contract with a private Care Management Organization (CMO) was awarded. The CMO will assume primary responsibility for the following functions under a risk-shared contract: creating medical necessity or service necessity criteria, preauthorizing and gatekeeping for certain care, ongoing utilization management, creating provider networks, contract management with providers, tracking outcomes and system performance indicators, case management, approving claims and billing and reimbursement, and collecting data to meet state and federal reporting requirements.

Financial Arrangements. Over the next three years, approximately 1,500 children and their families will participate in this demonstration, which has an allocated budget of $42 million. Funding comes from multiple departments including child welfare, psychiatric services, developmental disabilities, Medicaid, juvenile justice, and alcohol and drug services. The Center for Healthcare Strategies provided financial support for the planning process.

The Care Management Organization (CMO) will negotiate rates with providers in the network. The CMO will receive a case rate of $3,200 per child per month. This will cover all services. A financial bonus will be awarded dependent on postdisenrollment "success" for 120 days. During the 120-day period following disenrollment, the provider will be responsible for payment for up to 60 days of out-of-home care placement, if the child reenters care. The contract will also include a risk-limitation pool that will be funded at 3.84% of the case rate during the first year of the initiative and requires any savings to be reinvested into the system. Additionally, 85% of state resources must be directed toward treatment services.

A single Technical Support Organization (TSO) contract was awarded for data and financial management. The TSO will assist the multiple state agencies in monitoring the system at multiple levels. Payment will be made on a no-risk fee arrangement.

New York

The state has been granted a Title IV-E demonstration waiver to test (in up to ten districts) various managed care approaches to support system reform. The proposal has as its central theme the reduction of care days in the foster care system, and the use of flexible funding to expand the use of non-foster care services. Specific goals include a decrease in foster care placements, an increase in flexibility and quality of care, a decrease in reentry, expedited permanency, and an increased rate of transfer to less restrictive settings

Social service districts are not required to participate in the waiver to develop child welfare managed care plans. Changes in New York State Social Services law in 1995 granted social service districts the option of developing managed care or other alternative systems to provide child welfare services. The law required districts to submit a Child Welfare Managed Care Plan if they planned to modify the existing payment system, change case management, or apply to participate in the federal IV-E waiver demonstration.

There are numerous small pilots underway in many of New York's counties. For example, the recent GAO report mentioned initiatives in Albany County, which provide preventive services to 1,700 children and families, a countywide wraparound program serving Children with SED in or at risk of placement in Oneida County, and another wraparound program in Tompkins County for youth in residential placements. Many of these initiatives cover fewer than 50 children.

This preliminary report highlights two current, large New York City initiatives: 1) the Community Assistance Reinvestment Strategy for Child and Family Services in New York City, and 2) the Neighborhood-Based Services Initiative in the Bronx.

New York City Administration for Children's Services (ACS) Community Assistance Reinvestment Strategy for Child and Family Services (Title IV-E Waiver)

This five-year demonstration project will support the development of neighborhood-based models of care that are more comprehensive, better integrated, and responsive to the needs of residents in a targeted set of communities. A Title IV-E waiver will help New York State accelerate the development of these models.

Local districts must apply to participate in the demonstration project, and selected sites will develop plans that take full advantage of the flexibility afforded by the Title IV-E waiver. Although the final number of sites will be determined as the program unfolds, between five and 15 demonstration sites are anticipated. The selected sites will reflect a broad range of community characteristics, including community needs and resources, demographics, geographic location, and provider readiness.

The project will implement changes in how services are managed, delivered, financed, and contracted. It will allow savings from reduced foster care expenses to be reinvested in the child welfare system.

Goals. Central goals include decreasing length of stay in out-of-home care, improving client outcomes, increasing permanency in the shortest time possible, and increasing prevention efforts to better protect at-risk children. The Title IV-E waiver will allow the demonstration sites to design programs that explore alternative strategies for integrated neighborhood-based services that can successfully fulfill these goals.

Populations Served. Populations eligible for this initiative include children in custody and children at risk of entering custody served by child welfare agencies in the demonstration sites. To maintain a continuum of services, children and families currently receiving care from agencies that become part of a Community Assistance Reinvestment provider network will remain the responsibilities of that service agency regardless of what community the child is from or where she/he is served. The provider network will also be responsible for all services to children and families in the target community who come to the attention of the provider network during the course of the demonstration.

Services. Services include case management, family preservation and support services, permanency planning with families, kinship care, family foster care, treatment foster care, group care, residential care/treatment, adoption services, mental health and substance abuse services, and wraparound services.

Service decisions will be made based on the best interest of the children and families, even if the service needs of the client must be fulfilled outside the network.

Quality and Outcomes. Case conferences, case reviews, and utilization, cost, and performance data from MIS tracking systems will be used to monitor outcomes and quality requirements in the following areas:

- Criteria related to cost (must be cost neutral, based on actual Title IV-E expenditures experienced among comparison sites),
- Requirements to adhere to professional standards or licensing requirements, and
- An independent evaluation of the initiative/demonstration (will assess effects on child and family outcomes, systems level reforms, costs/benefits, and the implementation process).

Roles and Responsibilities. The public child welfare agency will retain responsibility for determining Title IV-E or Medicaid eligibility, ongoing utilization management, contracting with providers, tracking outcomes and system performance indicators, billing and reimbursement, collecting data to meet state and federal reporting requirements, and case management related to treatment planning, long-term care determination, and placement services.

Lead agency service providers will assume primary responsibility for case management related to permanency planning, case management of mental health and substance abuse treatment for children and families, and for the creation of provider networks.

Financial Arrangements. A capitated reimbursement rate will initially be based on anticipated costs of out-of-home care over the five-year demonstration. This rate can change based on ongoing performance evaluation in control sites. Payments to providers will be made prospectively, supporting the development of preventive and aftercare services in the community.

The risk-share contract requires the provider to reinvest potential profits into the child welfare system. The contract will require a risk insurance pool, and termination of demonstration operations may occur to protect providers against major financial loss.

Funding for this demonstration comes solely from child welfare funds.

Neighborhood-Based Services Initiative: The Borough of the Bronx

This initiative will fundamentally reform the existing child welfare system in the borough of the Bronx by creating neighborhood-based, community-oriented service systems. Children who need foster care will be placed within their own communities, when appropriate and feasible, so that they will not have to switch schools, leave friends, or lose contact with their families. In addition, support services and extended networks of care will also be located in the community, allowing maximum access to a range of services in the child's familiar environment. This initiative strongly encourages a closely integrated system of care in which providers develop formal relationships and linkages with each other to more fully realize a broad range of neighborhood-based services.

The initiative will employ the Family-to-Family model of services that encourages open communication and trust between prospective foster parents, adoptive families, and child welfare workers. This model uses common assessment criteria and problem-solving approaches to areas of concern. The City has released an RFP for the Borough of the Bronx. (It is expected that RFPs for the other boroughs and for specialized services will be issued)

Goals. Central goals include improving client outcomes, increasing permanency in the shortest time possible, eliminating service gaps, and maintaining children in their communities.

Populations Served. The city projects that approximately 27,500 children will receive services from the neighborhood-based service initiative during the upcoming 12 months.

Children in custody and their families and children at risk of placement are eligible for this initiative.

Services. Neighborhood-based services strive to improve safety for children through networks dedicated to detecting abuse and neglect, and to reduce separation trauma for children while enhancing the possibility, timeliness, and quality of permanency for the child. The following neighborhood-based services are included: permanency planning with families, kinship care, family foster care, treatment foster care, group care, residential care/treatment, mental health treatment, and independent living services. In certain circumstances, it may be necessary to provide specialized services for a limited number of children with severe physical, medical, or behavioral impairments outside the child's home neighborhood.

Quality and Outcomes. Utilization, cost, and performance data from MIS tracking systems will be used to monitor outcomes and quality requirements in the following areas:

- Outcomes related to child functioning,
- Outcomes related to family functioning,
- Outcomes related to achievement of permanency planning goals, and
- Outcomes related to recidivism/reentry.

Roles and Responsibilities. The child welfare agency will retain primary responsibility for determining Title IV-E or Medicaid eligibility, gatekeeping for certain care, ongoing utilization management, contracting with providers, tracking outcomes and system performance indicators, billing and reimbursement, case management, and collecting data to meet county and federal reporting requirements.

Financing. Forty-five percent of funds are from federal funding, 20% state funds, and 35% local funds. A not-for-profit MCE or provider, operating under a case rate, will create and manage community-based provider networks.

NORTH CAROLINA

North Carolina Child Welfare Waiver Demonstration

This demonstration is currently implementing changes in the management, delivery, financing, and contracting of child welfare services in 19 counties in the state. A Title IV-E federal waiver provides the state with the financial flexibility to connect system performance and system funding.

The Governor's office, the state legislature, the state child welfare and mental health agencies, nonprofit private providers, consumers, and child advocates were involved in the planning process.

Goals. Central goals include reducing the initial entry into the foster care system, decreasing length of stay in out-of-home care, increasing permanency in the shortest time possible, reducing the rate of reentry into care, and improving the system to match the child's vision of the child welfare system.

Populations Served. Populations eligible for this initiative include all children in custody and their families, adoptive families and children with adoption as the permanency goal, and families of children at risk of entering or reentering state custody or placement responsibility.

Services. Services include traditional and nontraditional services that can be directly associated with the goals of the demonstration.

Quality and Outcomes. Reports from families and providers and utilization, cost, and performance data from MIS tracking systems will be used to monitor quality requirements and outcomes in the following areas:

- Specific system performance indicators related to program effectiveness (number of kids substantiated as abused or neglected, pattern of placements including disruption and where they go, and the number of children who enter custody for the first time),

- Specific criteria related to cost (cost neutrality),

- Specific criteria related to appropriateness of services (pattern of placement, disruptions, and where children are placed),

- Outcomes related to achievement of permanency planning goals (length of stay, number of children who exit care as a result of adoption),

- Outcomes related to recidivism/reentry (rate of reentry, number of children with repeat resubstantiations, number of disruptions, proportion of children in foster care with a history of involvement with the system), and

- An independent evaluation of the initiative/demonstration (University of North Carolina will conduct).

Roles and Responsibilities. The state child welfare agency is primarily responsible for the management of the demonstration, including ongoing utilization management, tracking outcomes and system performance indicators, billing and reimbursement, and the collection of data for the purpose of meeting state and federal reporting requirements.

The participating counties may choose to contract with lead agencies, MCEs, or providers under whatever fee arrangement they negotiate, or they can elect to manage and provide services without sharing risks with providers.

Financial Arrangements. This initiative is dependent upon the funding flexibility provided by a Title IV-E waiver. Demonstration activities are supported by federal, state, and county funds.

The state expects the counties to achieve cost neutrality and allows the counties to place any money that they do not spend into "trust" accounts for improving and expanding services to achieve the goals of the demonstration.

Financial risk is increased for participating counties since they are operating within the limits of a financial cap. Buncombe County is highlighted.

Buncombe County, North Carolina

The Governor's Office, the state legislature, state and county child welfare agencies, state Medicaid and mental health agencies, county alcohol and drug abuse agency, Department of Education, nonprofit private providers, consumers, juvenile and family court, and local foundations were involved in planning this initiative.

Goals. Central goals include increasing permanency in the shortest time possible, increasing the safety and well-being of children, maintaining children in their communities, and increasing funding for wraparound and aftercare services.

Populations Served. All children in state/county custody, including those in out-of-home care, children in out-of-state or out-of-county arrangements, adoptive families and children with adoption as the permanency goal, children with SED, regardless of whether or not they are in custody, children served by child welfare agencies who are not in custody, families of children in custody or who are at risk of entering custody, and children involved with the juvenile justice system are eligible for inclusion in this initiative. The county projects that 3,403 children will be served during the upcoming year.

Services. Services include case management, child protective services intake and investigations, emergency shelter, family preservation and support services, day treatment, permanency planning with families, kinship care, family foster care, treatment foster care, group care, residential care/treatment, psychiatric hospitalization, adoption recruitment and services, postadoption subsidies and support, juvenile justice, mental health and substance abuse treatment for children and their families, wraparound services, respite care, and independent living.

Quality and Outcomes. Reports from families, providers, and schools; standardized assessments; pre- and post-tests; and utilization, cost and performance data from MIS tracking systems will be used to monitor quality requirements and outcomes in the following areas:

- System performance indicators related to program effectiveness,
- Cost neutrality,
- Specific criteria related to access/availability of services and utilization patterns (community board supports for families),
- Specific criteria related to appropriateness of services,
- Development of Level of Care criteria or clinical protocols,
- Consumer satisfaction requirement,
- Outcomes related to family functioning,
- Outcomes related to recidivism/reentry,
- Credentialing requirements for individual providers (Carolina Alternatives),
- Accreditation of agencies/facilities according to national standards (child care agency accreditation and system of care assessment),
- Specific criteria or standards related to cultural competence of providers or managed care entities, and
- An independent evaluation of the initiative.

Financial Arrangements. Medicaid and Title IV-E waivers will provide funding flexibility necessary to support this initiative.

The county plans to share financial risk with providers within the next year. The county child welfare administration will be responsible for negotiating a case rate with the providers. It has not been determined whether to include a risk adjustment mechanism or to limit the potential retained savings of the providers.

OHIO

The state is in the process of implementing ProtectOhio, a five-year Title IV-E waiver demonstration project. Fourteen of Ohio's 88 counties have elected to participate in the waiver demonstration. ProtectOhio is intended to reduce the number of children in foster care, decrease the time children remain in care, and promote adoptions. Through the demonstration, the state separates funding from utilization-based reimbursement. Federal and state foster care funds are combined with county funds and a capped allocation is prepaid to each participating county on a monthly basis. Funding for ProtectOhio FY 1999 is $49,015,476.04. This represents 9% of the total state child welfare budget.

Counties are given a great deal of flexibility in launching their programs. The county agency may act as a MCE, or contract out. Counties may elect to share risks with providers or MCEs, or not. The state gave guidance on broad outcomes required under the waiver, but counties had discretion to enhance what was required.

This report describes Lorain County, Cuyahoga County, Crawford County, Franklin County, and Hamilton County.

Crawford County

The state child welfare agency and the Family and Child First Council, a group of leaders representing mental health, drug and alcohol, juvenile court, health departments, county and city government, education, and MR/DD, were involved in planning this countywide initiative that is currently implementing changes in how services are managed, delivered, financed, and contracted. The Family and Child First Council must approve the placement of children into this managed care plan.

Goals. Central goals include decreasing the length of stay in out-of-home care, improving the quality of services, identifying and eliminating services gaps, and controlling, predicting, and limiting costs. The county predicts that 22 children will receive services under the authority of this initiative during the upcoming year.

Populations Served. Children and families in custody for the first time are eligible for this initiative, as are children in county custody who are in out-of-home placements outside the county.

Services. Services include case management, emergency shelter, family preservation and support services, day treatment, permanency planning with families, family foster care, treatment foster care, group care, residential care/treatment, psychiatric hospitalization, adoption recruitment, adoption services, mental health and substance abuse services for children and their families, wraparound and respite care, and independent living.

Quality and Outcomes. Reports from families, providers, and schools, and utilization, cost, and performance data from an MIS tracking system will be used to monitor quality requirements and outcomes in the following areas:

- System performance indicators related to program effectiveness,
- Criteria related to cost (the county will operate within the capped allocation it is awarded by the state),
- Credentialing requirements for individual providers (only licensed providers deliver services),
- Outcomes related to child and family functioning,
- Outcomes related to achievement of permanency planning goals (the child will return home for six months successfully), and
- Requirements to adhere to professional standards or licensing requirements (all placements and services are required to be state licensed).

Roles and Responsibilities. The county child welfare agency will retain primary responsibility for determining Title IV-E or Medicaid Waiver eligibility, preauthorizing care, gatekeeping for certain care, ongoing utilization management, contracting with a private managed care entity, tracking outcomes and system performance indicators, billing and reimbursement, and collecting data to meet state and federal reporting requirements.

A risk-share contract delegates responsibility to a for-profit lead agency for the following services: creating medical necessity or service necessity criteria, contracting with providers, creating provider networks, and case management for permanency planning, treatment planning, long-term care determination, placement services, and services to families for mental health or substance abuse treatment.

Financial Arrangements. The state and county child welfare agencies, the county mental health agency, and the Department of Juvenile Justice contribute funding to this initiative. The funding flexibility provided by the Title IV-E waiver also supports the efforts of this initiative, which represents approximately 10% of the total county child welfare budget.

Negotiations between the county child welfare agency and the for-profit lead agency resulted in a case rate of $38,500 per child, from the time of entry into care until the child returns home for six months successfully. The contract includes an aggregate stop-loss provision for the lead agency of $250,000.

Cuyahoga County: Managed Care Initiative (not a waiver county)

The county child welfare agency and nonprofit private providers have been involved in the planning of this countywide pilot and have made plans to implement changes in the management and finance of services. The initiative is developing a pilot assessment tool that can be used with children and families to determine the appropriate level of care, develop utilization review capacity and a case rate pilot, and measure outcomes/standards in private provider contracts.

Goals. Central goals include improving client outcomes, ensuring more efficient use of limited resources, better matching the level of care and level of need, and integrating the level of services provided to children and families.

Population Served. Up to 500 children in county custody and their families (up to 192) will be eligible for the case rate pilot.

Services. This initiative will include the development and use of a pilot assessment tool to determine the level of care for children and families. This measurement of outcomes and standards will be applied to the delivery of case management, day treatment, permanency planning with families, family foster care, treatment foster care, group care, residential care/treatment, and mental health and substance abuse treatment.

Quality and Outcomes. Utilization, cost, and performance data from a MIS tracking system and standardized assessments will be used to monitor the quality requirements and outcomes that are incorporated into this tool. The county has not yet determined what quality requirements and outcomes will be included since the tool is still under development.

Roles and Responsibilities. The county child welfare agency will retain primary responsibility for determining Title IV-E or Medicaid eligibility, ongoing utilization management, contracting with providers, tracking outcomes and system performance indicators, billing and reimbursement, and collecting data to meet state and federal reporting requirements.

However, the primary responsibility for case management services related to treatment planning, long-term care determination, placement services, and services to families for mental health or substance abuse treatment will be "passed" to a not-for-profit provider in the case rate pilot.

Financial Arrangements. Although a precise budget for the upcoming year has not been determined, the county expects to blend funding from child welfare, mental health, and Medicaid to support the services covered by this initiative. The county will provide 48% of the funding and federal funding will provide the remaining 52%.

Franklin County: Managed Care Contracting

The county child welfare agency, nonprofit private providers, and juvenile and family courts have been involved in planning this countywide initiative. The county released an RFP and selected three lead agencies; one agency has since withdrawn. The two remaining lead agencies are Ohio Youth Advocate Program and Permanent Family Solutions, with Buckeye Ranch as the lead. Implementation is scheduled for February 1, 1999.

Goals. Central goals include reducing the lengths of stay of children in out-of-home care, maintaining children in their own homes, achieving permanency sooner, and providing faster access to front-end services.

Populations Served. Populations eligible for this initiative include children in county custody (including those in out-of-home care), children with SED in custody and not in custody, children not in custody served by child welfare agencies, families of children in custody, families of children at risk of being in custody, and children involved with the juvenile justice system. The pilot will serve up to 1,000 children (500 cases), which represents approximately 15% of the current caseload in the county. This population will be drawn from a random sample of the populations listed above.

Services. Services include family preservation and support services, day treatment, permanency planning with families, kinship care, family foster care treatment foster care, group care, residential care/treatment, psychiatric hospitalization, juvenile justice, mental health and substance abuse treatment for children and families, wraparound services, respite care, and independent living.

Quality and Outcomes. Reports from families, standardized assessments, and utilization, cost, and performance data from an MIS tracking system will be used to monitor outcomes and quality requirements in the following areas:

- Specific system performance indicators related to program effectiveness (100% of children will experience no substantiated abuse or neglect while their case is open, 100% of children in paid placements will not experience abuse or neglect),

- Specific criteria related to cost (the establishment of a case rate with no time limit),
- Specific criteria related to access/availability (80% or more of children served will have face-to-face contact at least every 30 days, 90% or more of children will have face-to-face contact at least every 60 days),
- Specific criteria related to appropriateness of services:
  - at least 75% of children, ages 0-12 being served will live with their families,
  - at least 55% of children ages 13 and older being served will live with their families,
  - at least 55% of all children served will never enter custody during the span of their case, and
  - at least 85% of children in custody will be in a nonrestrictive placement.
- Development of Level of Care criteria or clinical protocols,
- Consumer satisfaction requirement
- Placement stability
  - no fewer than 45% leave care with only one placement (no moves),
  - no fewer than 25% leave care with two placements (one move),
  - no more than 12% of children experience three placements during custody (two moves), and
  - no more than 16% of children experience four or more placements during custody (three or more moves).
- Outcomes related to achievement of permanency planning goals
  - the median number of days that children spend in Temporary Custody should be no more than 85,
  - no more than 40% of children will remain in temporary custody for more than six months,
  - no more than 25% of children will remain in temporary custody after 12 months,
  - at least 80% of the children leaving custody will return to their families, and

- at least 75% of the children leaving custody will have spent less than one year in custody.

- Outcomes related to recidivism/reentry
  - no more than 7% of clients will experience substantiated or indicated abuse or neglect reports within six months of case closure,
  - no more than 12% of clients will experience substantiated or indicated abuse or neglect reports within 12 months of case closure, and
  - of children whose cases are closed each quarter, 8% or less will be opened within six months.

- Requirements to adhere to professional standards or licensing requirements,

- Credentialing requirements for individual providers, based on state laws and regulatory requirements,

- Accreditation of agencies/facilities according to national standards (COA accreditation is required for lead agencies), and

- Criteria or standards related to cultural competence of providers or managed care entities (requirement for training and policy).

In addition to the specific thresholds established by Franklin County and listed above, the county is considering monitoring other indicators on either a monthly or daily basis although a threshold has not yet been established. These include

- rate of deaths or injuries to children,
- rate of open cases with reports of abuse or neglect,
- rate of children hospitalized,
- lack of monthly face-to-face contact with children,
- number of days a child remains in temporary custody,
- increase in the level of risk as assessed on the ME-FRAM,
- parent visitation occurring less than indicated in the case plan,
- parent participation in the case plan,
- whether a Voluntary Protective Service case is open for longer than six months,
- whether a Court Order Protective Service case is open for longer than nine months,

- whether a temporary court custody case is open longer than 12 months,
- birth of a child while case is open,
- families who go "AWOL" and are not located within 30 days of last contact, and/or
- moves to a more restrictive placement that last for more than 14 days.

Roles and Responsibilities. Under this arrangement, the county child welfare agency will retain control of the following functions: determining Title IV-E or Medicaid eligibility, intake and investigation, contracting with lead agencies, tracking outcomes and system performance indicators, collecting data for the purpose of meeting state and federal reporting requirements, and case management related to permanency planning and long-term care determination.

The county plans to share financial risk with the lead agencies for the following functions: preauthorizing for care, gatekeeping for certain care, ongoing utilization management, creating provider networks and contract management with providers, and case management related to treatment planning and placement services.

Financial Arrangements. The project budget for the next 12 months is approximately $7.5 million dollars; this represents approximately 15% of the total county child welfare budget. The state has relied on the flexibility provided by the Title IV-E waiver to contract for new services for populations not allowable without a waiver. The financial risk-share arrangement the county plans to use will include a case rate and penalties related to outcome measurements/performance-based contracts. The amount of the case rate is under negotiation, but will be awarded *per case* for the length of services. The case rate will include a six-month past case closure stipulation and will include decreasing responsibility for the 18 months after closing. There is also a risk adjustment mechanism, which limits the amount a lead agency can lose or gain each year.

Hamilton County

Hamilton County has two initiatives—Creative Connections is designed for the county's most challenging, multisystem children, and TrueCare Partnership is the behavioral health plan for children and families with mental health or substance abuse needs from across the county, with referrals coming from child welfare, mental health, and substance abuse systems.

CREATIVE CONNECTIONS

The county child welfare and mental health agencies, the county alcohol and drug abuse agency, nonprofit private providers, the juvenile court, and the local MR/DD Board were involved in the planning and implementation process. The initiative is an agreement between the Hamilton County Family and Children First Council (the Council), a public entity created to carry out the child welfare mandates described in Ohio Revised Code and Beech Acres to transfer the primary responsibility for administering and delivering social services to troubled youth and includes the introduction of shared financial risk.

Goals. Central goals include improving client outcomes, controlling, predicting, and limiting costs, better matching level of care and level of need, and improving access to services for consumers.

Populations Served. Children served by multiple systems are eligible for this initiative. This includes children in county custody, including those in out-of-home or out-of-state or out-of-county placements, seriously emotionally disturbed children, and children involved with the juvenile justice system. The initiative serves the county's children with the most intensive needs: 358 children from 255 families each year. The number of enrollees should not be less than 286 at anytime unless the decrease is due to some factor other than the inability of Beech Acres to provide case management services.

Services. Services include case management, day treatment, family foster care, treatment foster care, group care, residential care/treatment, mental health services for children and their families, wraparound services, respite care, and mentoring.

Quality and Outcomes. Beech Acres and the county in-home services will use reports from families and providers, standardized assessments, pre- and post-tests, and utilization, cost, and performance data from MIS tracking systems to monitor outcomes and quality requirements in the following areas:

- Specific system performance indicators related to program effectiveness,
- Specific criteria related to cost (maximize Medicaid revenue, no increase in average cost per enrollee, and decreased individual outlier reimbursement),
- Specific criteria related to access/availability of services and utilization patterns (plans of care, amendments, and quarterly individual

enrollee progress reports are completed in a timely manner and meet the Quality Protocol),

- Specific criteria related to appropriateness of services
  - average and median number of days enrollees receive institutional treatment point-in-time base line data reported;
  - demonstrated decrease in number of days enrollees stay in institutional settings;
  - increased number and proportion of enrollees upon enrollment and four months later who are successfully stepped down to relative, foster home, community-based group home, or home setting; and
  - demonstrated increase in the number and proportion of enrollees successfully stepped down from out-of-home placements to less restrictive placements.
- Development of Level of Care criteria or clinical protocols,
- Consumer satisfaction requirement,
- Outcomes related to recidivism/reentry,
- Placement stability and appropriateness:
  - decreased rate of unplanned movement from and to each placement setting type,
  - decreased rate of placement moves to same or more restrictive placement settings, and
  - decreased rate of inpatient hospitalizations for enrollees in out-of-home care settings.
- Requirements to adhere to professional standards or licensing requirements,
- Decreased use of out-of-region institutional placement and decreased use of out-of-county foster care placement,
- An independent evaluation of the initiative (Beech Acres' aggregate data reports, measuring systems, and project policies are accurate, timely, and adequate in assisting the Council and Council agencies in meeting the goals of the project,
- Criteria for performance of MIS, and
- Criteria/standards related to performance/maintenance of provider networks.

Roles and Responsibilities. The county child welfare agency will retain primary responsibility for the following functions: determination of Title IV-E or Medicaid eligibility, tracking outcomes and system performance indicators, case management (shared with Beech Acres) related to permanency planning, long-term care determination, and the collection of data for the purpose of meeting state and federal reporting requirements.

The county has a risk-share contract with the not-for-profit lead agency, Beech Acres, to provide care management and gatekeeping for certain care, ongoing utilization management, contract management with providers in the networks, case management services for families for mental health or substance abuse treatment, claims approval, billing and reimbursement, and reporting fiscal and performance information to the county.

Financial Arrangements. This initiative represents 18% of the county's total child welfare spending and has an annual budget of $12.8 million. No budget changes are projected for the upcoming year. Child welfare, mental health, Medicaid, juvenile justice, substance abuse, and MR/DD funds are blended.

County public agencies provide $3,220 of the $3,730 per-child per-month case rate paid to Beech Acres. The remainder is funded by Medicaid, state cluster funds, and Beech Acres' own contribution. The total number of months per year shall not exceed 3,432 unless the number of enrollees and the rate are increased in accordance with the agreement procedure contained in the contract. The private nonprofit management entity is responsible for negotiating the rates with providers (or subcontractors) in the network.

The arrangement with Beech Acres includes individual and aggregate stop-loss risk-sharing:

> **Individual stop-loss:** if at any time the total actual cost of providing services to an individual enrollee exceeds $7,000 per month for three consecutive calendar months, for any calendar month following such three-month period, direct Service Costs between $7,001 and $15,000 per month shall be shared equally by Beech Acres and the Council. Any Direct Service Costs in excess of $15,000 per month after such three month period shall not be paid by Beech Acres or the Council, but Beech Acres shall negotiate leave to obtain funding for Direct Service Costs for an Enrollee

exceeding $15,000 per month through an individual agreement with the referring County Agency. If Beech Acres is unable to obtain such an Agreement with referring County Agency, Beech Acres may disenroll the Enrollee. Disenrollment under these circumstances shall not be deemed a violation of either the No-Eject/ No-Reject policy.

Aggregate stop-loss: The agreement also includes the following mechanism for limiting the potential total risk and annual profits for Beech Acres. Beech Acres is required to submit financial reports on a quarterly basis. If the annual project revenue is greater than project cost the difference will be designated as the "Annual Aggregate Financial Surplus" and the surplus will be apportioned as follows:

(a) if the Annual Aggregate Financial Surplus is $333,333 or less in Contract year One or $500,000 or less in Contract Years Two-Four, Beech Acres shall retain the entire Annual Aggregate Financial Surplus, and (b) Beech Acres and the Council shall share equally any amount of Annual Aggregate Financial Surplus above $333,333 in Contract Year One and above $500,000 in Contract Years Two-Four. The same formula applies to actual losses to Beech Acres.

The contract stipulates that the Council shall pay Beech Acres or Beech Acres shall pay the Council no later than November 30th (following the close of each contract year) the amount of the annual Aggregate Financial Deficit or the amount of the annual Aggregate Financial Surplus.

Additionally, the contract contained financial penalties that can be imposed if Beech Acres fails to meet performance standards that have been established and incorporated into the contract.

TRUECARE PARTNERSHIP: A BEHAVIORAL HEALTH SERVICES INITIATIVE

The largest managed care effort affecting child welfare services in Ohio is the TrueCare Partnership, which began in January 1998. Under a no-risk, ASO arrangement, the county contracted with a for-profit behavioral health organization to manage the behavioral health care for children and families in need of outpatient mental health services or foster care in therapeutic group or residential settings, and to build an information system for three county agencies—child welfare, mental health, and alcohol and drug addiction.

The state and county child welfare agencies, state Medicaid agency, state and county mental health agencies, state and county alcohol and drug abuse agencies, nonprofit private providers, juvenile and family court, and guardians were involved in the planning and implementation process.

Goals. Central goals include improving client outcomes; controlling, predicting, and limiting costs; better matching level of care and level of need; and improving access to services for consumers.

Populations Served. All children in county custody, including those in out-of-home, out-of-county, or out-of-state care who have an SED need; adoptive families and children with adoption as the permanency goal who have SED needs; children with SED, regardless of whether or not they are in custody; families of children with SED in custody or at risk of entering custody; and children with SED involved with other community agencies are eligible for this initiative.

Approximately 3,200 children received services last year, or about 35 % of the county's child welfare population.

Services. Services include case management, day treatment, treatment foster care, group care, residential care/treatment, postadoption subsidies and support, outpatient mental health services for children and their families, independent living, and mentoring.

Quality and Outcomes. The state will use reports from families and providers, standardized assessments, pre- and post-tests, and utilization, cost, and performance data from MIS tracking systems to monitor outcomes and quality requirements in the following areas:

- Specific system performance indicators related to program effectiveness (the continuity of care for services provided, ensure child safety and reduce the risk of harm),
- Specific criteria related to cost,
- Specific criteria related to access/availability of services and utilization patterns (children and families will receive timely behavioral health services, services are available to meet the needs of children and families),
- Specific criteria related to appropriateness of services (services are appropriate to the needs of children and families and provided in the least restrictive setting),
- Development of Level of Care criteria or clinical protocols,

- Consumer satisfaction requirement (children and family will accept and participate in family-centered services,
- Outcomes related to recidivism/reentry,
- Requirements to adhere to professional standards or licensing requirements,
- Specific criteria or standards related to cultural competence of providers or managed care entities,
- An independent evaluation of the initiative,
- Criteria for performance of MIS, and
- Criteria/standards related to performance/maintenance of provider networks.

Roles and Responsibilities. The county child welfare agency retains primary responsibility for determination of Title IV-E or Medicaid eligibility; gatekeeping for certain care; tracking outcomes and system performance indicators; case management related to permanency planning, long-term care determination, treatment, and placement planning; contract management; and the collection of data for the purpose of meeting state and federal reporting requirements.

Under a no-risk ASO contract, Magellan Public Solutions assumes primary responsibility for the following functions: creating medical necessity or service necessity criteria, gatekeeping for certain care, ongoing utilization management, contracting with providers and creating provider networks, case management services for families for mental health or substance abuse treatment, and billing and reimbursement. Magellan is responsible for assessments, training, and overall care management.

To meet its ASO responsibilities, Magellan subcontracted with four other companies to manage outpatient mental health services (Green Springs Health Services), to maximize Medicaid revenue and handle claims processing oversight (Public Consulting Group), and to provide the hardware for the MIS functions and manage the software and network (CMHC Systems, Inc. and Kandl Data Products). To fulfill its service delivery responsibilities, Magellan has subcontracted with 22 local providers. At the end of five years, the county intends to assume responsibility for the initiative. The county will assume responsibility earlier if Magellan's performance is not satisfactory.

Financial Arrangements. Child welfare, mental health, and Medicaid dollars are contributed to the budget for this initiative. The county estimates that $13 million was spent on this initiative during the past 12 months and projects that $14 million will be spent during the upcoming 12 months. A Title IV-E waiver allows for funding flexibility that supports some of the activities of this initiative. The state has applied for a Medicaid waiver that is still pending.

The county does not currently share financial risk with Magellan, but is planning to introduce risk-sharing arrangements with both the ASO and providers in the future. The county has not determined the method that will be used to share risk, but is considering establishing performance-based contracts that include bonuses related to the achievement of specific outcome measurements.

Lorain County: Integrated Services Partnership

The Integrated Services Partnership is a countywide initiative that is currently implementing changes in the management and delivery of services. There are plans to implement changes in financing, contracting, and management within one year. The Partnership is an outgrowth of the children's cluster that began pooling funds and combining efforts from various interest groups and departments (Lorain County children services, schools, mental health, court of domestic relations, juvenile justice, MR/DD, and the addiction recovery services) to reduce the number of children in residential care and to better utilize community resources to prevent placement. Lorain County participated in a national collaborative project, funded in part by the Casey Foundation, that facilitated the expansion of the client population to include disenfranchised youth.

An RFP was released and the contract has been awarded to Pressley Ridge to implement the Integrated Services Partnership initiative.

Goals. Central goals include improving client outcomes, decategorizing or "pooling funding" to create a more seamless system of care, maintaining children in their communities, and decreasing out-of-home care placement.

Populations Served. Populations eligible for this initiative include all children in state/county custody, children in out-of-state or out-of-county placements, children with SED in custody, children with SED not in custody, children served by child welfare agencies who are not in custody, families of children at risk of entering custody, and children involved with the juvenile justice system.

During the past year, the pilot served 23 children from seven families. The county has not provided an estimate of the number of children to be served during the upcoming year.

Services. Services include case management, family preservation and support services, treatment foster care, group care, residential care, juvenile justice, behavioral health services and treatment for children and families, wraparound services, and respite care.

Quality and Outcomes. Reports from families and providers; utilization, cost, and performance data from MIS tracking systems; and client satisfaction surveys will be used to monitor quality requirements and outcomes in the following areas:

- System performance indicators related to program effectiveness (95% of incidents involving the child are successfully dealt with by the Partnership, provider panel and care management team, and Intersystem of Care has Quality Assurance structure and policies and procedures to safeguard quality of care),

- Criteria related to cost (the average cost per episode of care cannot exceed current levels, and attain a 5% Department of Youth Services placement reduction for the county),

- Criteria related to access/availability of services and utilization patterns:

  - 95% of calls returned within one day;
  - 95% of all emergency pager calls responded to within 30 minutes;
  - 95% of all routine pages required within 90 minutes;
  - 95% of assessments will be completed within seven days;
  - documented attempts to contact all community treatment team members within 24 hours of referral;
  - 98% of care managers assigned within required time frames, with the rest assigned within two days;
  - 95% of services available within required time frames;
  - 90% of all youth identified as needing assessment will have a comprehensive domain assessment with service recommendations within seven working days; and

- 100% of all youth identified as needing specialized assessments, e.g., Chemical Dependency Assessment, Sexual Offending Risk Assessment, will have the assessment completed within ten days.
- Criteria related to appropriateness of services:
  - 95% compliance with the Partnership's protocols;
  - no provider will move or discharge a child without prior Intersystem of Care approval, unless the child or other children's safety is a imminent risk;
  - development of respite beds; and
  - percentage of children leaving out-of-home care who are increasing with level of care.
- Consumer satisfaction requirement (that 90% of consumers show satisfaction with the Intersystem of Care by scoring a "3" or better on client satisfaction survey),
- Outcomes related to child functioning (based on before and after comparisons using standardized functional scales [CAFAS] and percent of children in therapeutic placements who are "absent without leave" within a three-month period),
- Outcomes related to family functioning,
- Outcomes related to achievement of permanency planning goals:
  - placement is not reason for continued stay in more than 5% of cases;
  - frequency and percent of children receiving treatment being maintained at home, with a relative or family placement, and not requiring a more restrictive placement;
  - develop baseline regarding percent of children who leave out-of-home care treatment who remain in a stable, less restrictive setting (including home); and
  - percentage of children returning home within six months.
- Outcomes related to recidivism/reentry:
  - documentation of the frequency and type of indicated and substantiated child abuse investigations at treatment facilities, and in the community;
  - less than 10% increase in level of care once discharged from placement, within a six-month period; and

- percentage of children and adolescents who maintain in placement for six months after discharge from a more restrictive placement.
- Accreditation of agencies/facilities according to national standards (COA or JCAHO), and
- Criteria or standards related to cultural competence of providers or managed care entities:
  - inclusion of cultural competency as a standard in provider credentialing,
  - 100% of staff are trained in cultural competency, and
  - 95% of consumers report satisfaction with staff's cultural sensitivity and competence.

Pressley Ridge, the not-for-profit lead agency that was awarded the no-risk contract, is primarily responsible for the following services: determining Title IV-E or Medicaid eligibility, creating medical necessity or service necessity criteria, gatekeeping for certain care, ongoing utilization management, contracting with providers and creating provider networks, tracking outcomes and system performance indicators, case management, and collecting data for the purpose of meeting state, county, and federal reporting requirements.

Lorain County does not plan to share risks with the contractor during the first year of the contract. The funding will be provided by the county departments of child welfare, mental health, juvenile justice, addiction recovery services, and MR/DD. It is anticipated that risk-sharing will begin in the second year of the contract.

OKLAHOMA

Children's Services Initiative

This statewide initiative changed the management and delivery of services for children at risk of disrupted placements and children soon to be reunited with their families. The state released an invitation to bid, approved proposals, completed implementation, and is concurrently completing an evaluation and monitoring process.

The state legislature, child welfare agency, Medicaid agency, mental health agency, and alcohol and drug abuse agency, nonprofit private providers, and consumers have been involved in the planning process.

Goals. Central goals include improving client outcomes and the quality of services, allowing providers the flexibility to provide individualized and accessible care, and identifying and eliminating service gaps.

Populations Served. Populations eligible for this initiative include children in out-of-home care arrangements who are at risk of placement disruption, adoptive families and children with adoption as the permanency goal who are at risk of placement disruption, children who are served by child welfare agencies but are not in custody, families of children in custody or are at risk of entering custody, children in kinship care at risk of placement disruption, and children who will be reunified with biological families within 30-90 days of referral for service.

A total of 2,500 families, and approximately 3,700 children, are affected by this initiative. Child welfare staff must refer children and families for them to be eligible for inclusion in the initiative.

Services. Services provided could include case management, family preservation and support, permanency planning, mental health (only if a particular provider is a community mental health clinic), substance abuse treatment for children, wraparound services, independent living, home-based supportive services, parent education, fiscal and household management, educational advocacy and linkage, and supportive counseling.

Additionally, a special pilot in one of eight service (geographic) areas of the state will provide drug testing for parents.

Quality and Outcomes. Reports from families and providers; standardized assessments; pre- and post-tests; utilization, cost, and performance data from MIS tracking systems; and annual onsite program visits will be used to monitor outcomes and quality requirements in the following areas:

- Specific system performance indicators related to program effectiveness (based on outcome of families career with this initiative),
- Costs for service are up to $3,000 per family and up to $400 for other concrete goods and services per family,
- Criteria related to access to services (children at risk of out-of-home placement, children at risk of placement disruption, and children who are being reunified in 30-90 days),
- Specific criteria related to appropriateness of services,
- Development of Level of Care Criteria or clinical protocols,
- Consumer satisfaction requirement (a client satisfaction survey is administered),

- Outcomes related to child functioning (use of a Family Intervention Plan),
- Outcomes related to family functioning (use of a Family Intervention Plan),
- Outcomes related to the achievement of permanency planning goals (use of a Family Intervention Plan),
- Outcomes related to recidivism/reentry (this will be tracked through the state's KIDS information system),
- Requirements to adhere to professional standards or licensing requirements,
- Specific criteria or standards related to cultural competence of providers or managed care entities,
- An independent evaluation of the initiative (an evaluation team from University of Oklahoma Health Sciences Center will complete an independent evaluation), and
- Monthly service utilization and documentation completion (monitoring reports must be submitted monthly with request for payment or payment is not processed).

Roles and Responsibilities. The state child welfare agency will retain primary responsibility for the following functions: ongoing utilization management, tracking outcomes and system performance indicators, billing and reimbursement, and contracting with providers.

The county child welfare agency will have primary responsibility for the remaining functions. These include determination of Title IV-E or Medicaid eligibility, case management, and the collection of data for the purpose of meeting state and federal reporting requirements.

The providers were responsible for creating their own networks prior to competing for the contract. There is only one provider that is also a community mental health clinic; this is the only provider that is able to pre-authorize care for their clients. All others must go through the Oklahoma Foundation for Medical Quality based on Relative Value Units (RVU), which are units of service per type of treatment, from the Client Assessment Record (CAR) form. This assessment process determines the units of service that a client should/could receive based on the severity of need.

Financial Arrangements. The state plans to share financial risk with providers, but not during the next year. The state is considering using a rate of $400 per family per month for up to six months. This may be broken down into a daily rate based on a seven-day-a-week schedule. The state child welfare administration will establish the final rate based on current utilization costs, the number of families being served, and the average duration of services.

During the past year, $7.2 million was used for this initiative. The state projects that $7.2 million plus Medicaid funds will support this initiative during the upcoming year.

Neither a Title IV-E nor Medicaid waiver supports this initiative. However, providers are able to draw down Medicaid funding to enhance the array of services they can provide and are encouraged to tap into foundation or other private monies, as available.

The state is also expanding the services for children in out-of-home placement whose goal is to return home. In the event a child is removed with a goal to return home, home-based services can be "plugged in" for up to one year after reunification. The thought is to capitalize on the momentum and crisis surrounding removal as a catalyst for (positive) change and immediately work toward reunification. If unsuccessful, by month nine (third quarterly report), there should be sufficient information to move toward termination of parental rights.

PENNSYLVANIA

The state did not report any current statewide managed care or privatization initiatives related to child welfare services. However, the state does support pilots that are underway in various counties. An initiative in Berk County is described.

Berk County: Berkserve

Berkserve is a countywide demonstration pilot serving a small number of children and families. The initiative is currently implementing changes in how services are managed and delivered and plans to implement changes in financing and contracting within one year. The county child welfare agency, nonprofit private providers, and the juvenile and family courts were involved in planning this initiative.

Goals. Central goals include decreasing the length of stay in out-of-home care, ensuring more efficient use of limited resources, decategorizing or "pooling funding" to create a more seamless system of care, and maintaining children in their communities.

Populations Served. Children in state/county custody and children in custody in out-of-home care are eligible for this initiative.

During the past year, four children and two families were served by this initiative. The county projects that a minimum of 30 children from 15 families will receive services during the upcoming year.

Services. The initiative will include the delivery of case management, family preservation and support services, permanency planning with families, family foster care, group care, residential care/treatment, mental health services to children and families, substance abuse treatment services to children and families, wraparound services, and respite care.

Quality and Outcomes. Reports from families and providers and utilization, cost, and performance data from an MIS tracking system will be used to monitor outcomes and quality requirements in the following areas:

- Specific system performance indicators related to program effectiveness,
- Specific criteria related to access/availability of services and utilization patterns,
- Specific criteria related to appropriateness of services based on standardized protocols,
- Consumer satisfaction,
- Outcomes related to achievement of permanency planning goals,
- Outcomes related to recidivism/reentry, and
- Credentialing requirements for individual providers.

Roles and Responsibilities. The county child welfare agency will retain primary responsibility for determination of Title IV-E or Medicaid eligibility, gatekeeping for certain care, collecting data to meet county and federal reporting requirements, case management related to treatment planning, long-term care determination, and placement services.

Under a no-risk arrangement, the county will contract with a management service organization (MSO) and a local nonprofit lead agency to develop service necessity criteria, pre-authorize care, provide ongoing utilization management, create provider networks and manage contracts, track outcomes and system performance indicators, case management related to permanency planning and behavioral health services, claims approval, and billing and reimbursement.

Financial Arrangements. The entirety of the funding for this initiative is drawn from the child welfare budget. Ninety percent of the funding is provided by state and federal funds and the remaining 10% by county funds. Regulatory waivers were procured to allow private providers to case manage and undertake documentation roles previously the sole responsibility of county staff.

The initiative does not currently, but plans to share financial risk with service providers during its second phase by contracting a case rate per family for all services included in the initiative. The rate will be established based on experience and information gathered during the first year of the demonstration, and the contract will be negotiated by a private managed care entity and the county child welfare administration. The contract will include a risk adjustment mechanism, but this has not yet been developed. The county has not yet determined whether there will be limitations on the use of potential savings or profits for providers and managed care organizations involved in this demonstration.

SOUTH CAROLINA

Privatized Adoption Services

The state released an RFP for adoption services in late summer 1998. The state Department of Social Services (DSS) proposes to award contracts for each of its seven regions. Awards had not been made at the time the survey was conducted. The RFP calls for private nonprofit, licensed agencies to provide recruitment, training, and assessment of prospective adoptive families and to coordinate the placement and postplacement services for all children referred. The contract is for 12 months, with up to four annual renewals.

Goals. Central goals include decreasing length of stay in out-of-home care by expediting adoption placements for children with adoption as the permanency goal, and ensuring stability of adoptive placements before and after finalization.

Population. The department may refer any child with special needs who has adoption as the permanent plan, is not in a foster home where the plan is adoption by that family, has no identified family, and where one of the following conditions exist: the child is legally free for adoption, the TPR has been filed, or one parent has relinquished rights and it is determined that the rights of the other parent will be terminated within the next 12 months. The state anticipates that 200 to 250 children will be served annually.

Services. The contractor and any subcontractors will recruit, train, assess, and prepare prospective adoptive families, complete adoptive home studies, provide placement and postplacement services, coordinate access to adoptive subsidy when appropriate, case manage specialized medical or behavioral health evaluations and services, provide transportation as needed to access services, participate in court reviews and foster care review boards, provide postadoption services for up to six months after final decree.

Quality and Outcomes. The contractors are required to meet specified Standards for Adoption services and all DSS policies and state and federal requirements. The Standards specify:

- Qualifications of agency personnel and credentials of those providing direct adoption services,
- Requirements related to training of staff and adoptive parents,
- Maximum caseload requirements,
- Quality standards for service planning (service plans within 30 days, updated every six months), and
- The contractor must document in quarterly reports (monthly face-to-face contacts with the child and adult members of adoptive family, description of services provided and appropriateness of services, and progress made toward finalization of plan).

Roles and Responsibilities. The state retains responsibility for maintaining legal custody of the child, making referrals of all eligible children and providing the eligible list electronically to all contractors, paying contractors according to the schedule in the contract, participating in case planning conferences at key decision points, determining eligibility for benefits, including Title IV-E and Medicaid, executing all adoptive subsidy agreements, approving or denying adoptive placements and consenting to adoptive finalization, and making final decisions in cases of disagreement about whether/when to disrupt an adoptive placement.

The contractor shall meet all standards and indicators in the Standards for Adoption Services and all requirements contained in the contract regarding case documentation.

Financial Arrangement. The maximum amounts payable under this contract are $13,000 per child or $15,700 per sibling group. The state will reimburse contractors based on the following schedule:

- The contractor receives $3,000 at the time a child or sibling group is placed in an adoptive or pre-adoptive home.

- The contractor is paid $375 for each month, up to a maximum of $4,500 for up to 12 months after the placement, during the time the contractor is supervising the placement. In the case of a sibling group, the monthly payment shall be $600 up to a maximum of $7,200.

- DSS pays any board payments or adoption subsidies or benefits per the foster or adoption agreement signed with the adoptive or pre-adoptive parent. These payments are made directly to the family by DSS.

- The contractor is paid $4,000 when the final adoption decree is received.

- The contractor is paid the remaining $1,500 six months after the final decree if the adoptive placement is still intact. Upon request of the family, the contractor will provide postadoptive services to children for up to six months after the final decree.

- The state may, at its option, reimburse contractor for placement supervision in an approved pre-adoptive home after the first 12 months at the rate of $350 per month for up to an additional six months if DSS believes the TPR and/or appeal will be concluded at the end of the six month period.

- If a family recruited by the contractor requests or agrees to accept a high legal risk child for a pre-adoptive placement by DSS, the contractor may agree to transfer the family's records to DSS and be reimbursed $3,500 for the recruitment and home study costs incurred by the contractor. That payment shall be made within 45 days after a child is placed with the family. If no placement is made, the contractor will receive no reimbursement.

- Lastly, if a family recruited by the contractor requests to become a DSS foster family for the placement of any foster children, the contractor may agree to transfer the family's records to DSS and be reimbursed $3,500 for the recruitment and home study costs. Payment will be made within 45 days after DSS places a child in the home.

Contractors were required to demonstrate sufficient financial reserves to operate for up to six months without payment from DSS.

TENNESSEE

The state reported two initiatives: 1) the Nonresidential Network, and 2) the Continuum of Care Contracts.

The state has released an RFP for six geographic regions or counties since the survey was completed. These regions include Davidson County, Mid-Cumberland Region, Northwest Region, Shelby County, South Central Region, and the Southwest Region. The Managed Care Institute plans to release information summarizing the details of these initiatives.

Nonresidential Network

This initiative is currently changing how nonresidential services are managed, delivered, financed, and contracted. The Governor's Office, state legislature, state child welfare agency, state Medicaid agency, state juvenile justice agency, nonprofit private providers, consumers, and local foundations were involved in planning this initiative.

Goals. Central goals include improving client outcomes, improving the quality of services, decreasing out-of-home care placement, and decategorizing or "pooling funds."

Population Served. Populations eligible for this initiative include children served by child welfare agencies who are not in custody, families of children in state custody and families of children at risk of entering custody, and children involved with the juvenile justice system.

Currently, only half of the state has been included in the initiative, the other half will be transitioned in by July 1, 1999.

Services. Services include case management, family preservation and support, respite care, and wraparound services.

Quality and Outcomes. Reports from families, providers, and schools, independent and department monitoring, and family satisfaction surveys will be used to monitor quality requirements and outcomes in the following areas:

- Specific system performance indicators related to program effectiveness,
- Specific criteria related to cost,
- Specific criteria related to appropriateness of services,
- Outcomes related to recidivism/reentry, and
- Credentialing requirements for individual providers.

Roles and Responsibilities. The state child welfare agency retains primary responsibility for all child welfare services included in the initiative.

However, the state child welfare agency shares responsibility for case management with providers.

Financial Arrangements. There will be financial risk sharing with providers in the form of required admissions and cooperative discharge agreements.

Continuum of Care Contracts

This statewide initiative has changed how services are delivered, financed, and contracted. The Governor's Office, state legislature, state child welfare agency, state Medicaid agency, state juvenile justice agency, nonprofit private provider, and consumers were involved in planning this initiative. In the upcoming year, the initiative will increase contracts to establish a system for permanency and reunification services.

Goals. Central goals include decreasing length of stay in out-of-home care, ensuring placement in the least restrictive level of care, increasing permanency in the shortest time possible, and providing individualized and accessible care.

Populations Served. Populations eligible for this initiative include all children in state custody, including children in out-of-home care, adoptive families and children with adoption as the permanency goal, and children involved with the juvenile justice system. Approximately 2,500 children are served annually.

Services. Services include case management, permanency planning with families, treatment foster care, group care, and residential care.

Quality and Outcomes. Reports from families, providers, and schools; standardized assessments; independent and departmental monitoring; and utilization, cost, and performance data from MIS tracking systems will be used to monitor quality requirements and outcomes in the following areas:

- Specific system performance indicators related to program effectiveness,
- Specific criteria related to cost,
- Specific criteria related to access/availability of services and utilization patterns,
- Development of Level of Care criteria or clinical protocols,
- Consumer satisfaction requirement,
- Outcomes related to child functioning,
- Outcomes related to family functioning,

- Outcomes related to achievement of permanency planning goals,
- Requirements to adhere to professional standards or licensing requirements,
- Credentialing requirements for individual providers, and
- An independent evaluation of the initiative/demonstration.

Roles and Responsibilities. The state child welfare agency retains primary responsibility for all of the services and administrative functions.

Financial Arrangements. The state is currently sharing financial risk with providers through a case rate equal to the rate offered by the state for service type and through increasing business to providers based on their success.

TEXAS

Project PACE (Permanency Achieved Through Coordinated Efforts)

The state legislature, state child welfare agency, state Medicaid agency, nonprofit private providers, children's services advocacy organizations, and child welfare-related services agencies participated in planning Project Permanency Achieved Through Coordinated Efforts (PACE).

The Texas Department of Protective and Regulatory Services released an RFP and awarded a contract to Lena Pope Home, Inc., to function as the lead agency to coordinate the delivery of certain child welfare services in a ten-county area in the Fort Worth region of the state.

Goals. Central goals include improving client outcomes, ensuring more efficient use of limited resources, decreasing lengths of stay, and reducing the number of moves children experience while in care through the delivery of coordinated services.

Population Served. The populations primarily eligible for this initiative are children in state custody with therapeutic needs and their families from the designated region. The State anticipates it will serve 200 children annually.

Services. Services delivered by the lead agency include emergency services, therapeutic foster care, residential care/treatment, substance abuse treatment for children, therapy, independent living services, family involvement services, and assessment services.

Quality and Outcomes. Reports from providers, standardized assessments, pre- and post-tests, contract monitoring, and utilization, cost, and performance data from MIS tracking systems will be evaluated to monitor quality requirements and outcomes in the following areas:

- System performance indicators related to program effectiveness (measured by changes in child functioning relative to level when entering care, fewer moves while in care, and reduced time in care),
- Criteria related to cost,
- Specific criteria related to access/availability of services and utilization patterns,
- Specific criteria related to appropriateness of services/based on standardized levels of care,
- Level of Care criteria,
- Consumer satisfaction requirement based on survey of children and caregivers,
- Outcomes related to child functioning (improvements in level of care of child),
- Outcomes related to achievement of treatment planning goals,
- Requirements to adhere to professional standards or licensing requirements,
- Credentialing requirements for individual providers,
- Specific criteria or standards related to cultural competence of providers, and
- An independent evaluation of the initiative/demonstration.

Roles and Responsibilities. Lena Pope Home, Inc., a not-for-profit agency, has primary responsibility for creating provider network and contract management with providers, claims approval and reimbursement, providing or coordinating assessment services, treatment planning, therapy, family involvement, and placement services.

The state child welfare agency retains primary responsibility for determining Title IV-E eligibility, creating service plans, Level of Care determination and gatekeeping for care, ongoing utilization management (through a contracted third party), tracking outcomes and system performance indicators, billing and reimbursement, collecting data to meet state and federal reporting requirements, and case management related to permanency planning.

Financial Arrangements. This initiative will be funded entirely from the child welfare budget. The pilot requires cost neutrality. Project PACE, Phase II, is tentatively intended to utilize a Title IV-E waiver to allow increased flexibility in service provision and payment options, but is not projected to begin implementation until approximately two years after the inception of Phase I. When fully implemented, the projected distribution of contributions are 45% state funds, 25% Title IV-E federal funds, and 30% TANF.

The lead agency, Lena Pope Home, Inc., will receive $72.40 per child per day to cover out-of-home care placement and maintenance costs, regardless of the Level of Care (LOC) of the child. This represents an average of the full LOC rates for contracted 24-hour out-of-home care in the Dallas-Fort Worth region. Lena Pope Home, Inc., and providers in the network will be required to use Medicaid funds to the greatest extent possible to supplement the case rate and support the therapeutic services and assessment services provided.

The state hopes to move from a flat per diem rate to a case rate, pending approval of a Texas Title IV-E waiver proposal. Presently, the state has not determined what the case rate might include or what risk adjustment mechanisms might be used.

UTAH

Residential Contract Restructuring

The state's child welfare agency, Medicaid agency, mental health agency, nonprofit private providers, youth corrections, and finance agency were involved in planning this initiative. The state has released an RFP and approved proposals for this statewide initiative to change the management and financing of residential services for 1,800 with SED needs in the state.

Goals. Central goals include ensuring more efficient use of limited resources, improving quality of services, providing individualized and accessible care, and controlling, predicting, and limiting costs.

Populations Served. Populations eligible for this initiative include children in state custody who are in out-of-home care, seriously emotionally disturbed children in state custody, and children involved with the juvenile justice system. The state projects that 1,800 children will participate in this initiative during the upcoming year.

Services. Services include day treatment, family foster care, treatment foster care, group care, residential care/treatment, mental health treatment, wraparound services, and independent living skill building services.

Quality and Outcomes. Reports from providers, reports from schools, standardized assessments, and measurement processes designed and described by providers will be used to monitor outcomes and quality requirements in the following areas:

- Criteria related to cost (a differential payment based on the maintenance and quality of staff has been proposed),
- Outcomes related to child functioning, and
- Outcomes measures established by providers in their RFPs (the RFP asked providers to set their own outcome measures and methods for measurements and rated the proposals based on these plans).

Roles and Responsibilities. The state child welfare agency will retain primary responsibility for determining Title IV-E or Medicaid eligibility, case management, gatekeeping for certain care, ongoing utilization management, contracting with providers, tracking outcomes and system performance indicators, billing and reimbursement, and collecting data to meet state and federal reporting requirements. A private provider will assume responsibility for creating medical necessity or service necessity criteria and preauthorizing care under a risk-shared contract. An exception is made when the provider is seeking care and/or services outside of the spectrum of services included in the level of care a child has been assigned. In this case, the state is responsible for pre-authorization.

Financial Arrangements. The state projects that $45 million will be spent for out-of-home care during the next 12 months. Medicaid, child welfare, mental health, and juvenile justice will contribute funding to this initiative. The state plans to negotiate contracts with providers within the year that will establish a daily case rate based on historical utilization and expenditures. The amount of the case rate will vary by the level of care the child is assigned and will range from approximately $56 to $227 per day.

WASHINGTON

Through a recently approved Title IV-E demonstration waiver, the Children's Administration in Washington State is experimenting with a "managed care" approach for the state's most challenging, resource-intensive children. The state is proposing to collaborate with other service delivery systems in selected demonstration sites to provide a comprehensive package of services for these children.

Title IV-E Waiver: Capitated Payment for Children with Special Needs

A September press release from the U.S. Department of Health and Human Services described the initiative as follows,

> The State of Washington will use federal foster care funds to provide comprehensive, individualized services to children 8 to 17 who are in need of mental health or special education services and are likely to be referred to group care. To avoid group assignments, the state will contract with local service providers to create and implement individualized treatment plans. The state will gauge the impact of the fixed case rate approach which allows services to be tailored to meet the complex needs of these children and their families at a reasonable cost.

Goals. The demonstration is intended to test the impact of financing mechanisms for specific services for identified populations, prevent group care placement, decrease length of stay in group care, and ensure placement of eligible children in least restrictive placements.

Populations. Children aged 8-17, who are likely to enter group care and are already involved with the mental health or special education systems for comprehensive services are eligible for this initiative. The demonstration will begin with Spokane County. Up to nine more counties may be added over five years. The initial site begins in early 1999. Approximately 380 children will be included in the Spokane County demonstration, with up to 620 additional children included as other counties participate.

Services. Services include in-home services and the full array of out-of-home care options to ensure that children can be placed in least restrictive settings in their own communities whenever placement is needed. Networks will include access to a variety of family support and therapeutic services to keep children safe in their own homes.

Financial Arrangements. The state will pay fixed rates to Regional Support Networks to provide all services needed by the eligible children and families who are referred to the demonstration. (No other financial information is available.)

WEST VIRGINIA

Region IV Foster Care Pilot Project

The state child welfare agency, state mental health agency, nonprofit private providers, the Child Welfare League of America, and a school of social work from the state were involved in planning this initiative. A contract is under negotiation and the state will implement changes in the management, financing, and contracting of services within the year.

Goals. Central goals include improving client outcomes, ensuring more efficient use of limited resources, improving quality of services, and better matching level of care and level of need.

Populations Served. Populations eligible for this initiative include children in certain out-of-home care arrangements, adoptive families and children with adoption as the permanency goal, and families of children in state custody. The initiative is limited to the southeastern region of the state. The state estimates that 400 children will be served during the upcoming year.

Services. Services include family foster care, treatment foster care, adoption recruitment, and adoption services.

Quality and Outcomes. Pre- and post-tests and utilization, cost, and performance data from MIS tracking systems will be used to monitor quality requirements and outcomes in the following areas:

- Specific criteria related to cost, and
- Credentialing requirements for individual providers (foster parent training certification).

Roles and Responsibilities. The state child welfare agency will retain primary responsibility for the administration, management, and delivery of services included in this initiative.

Financial Arrangements. The state child welfare agency will provide the entirety of the funding for this initiative and plans to use contracts that share financial risk with service providers within the year. The state has not determined the method that will be used to share risk with providers, but plans to use audits, research, and cost analysis to determine rates.

WISCONSIN

Wisconsin is a county-administered state, with the exception of Milwaukee County, which is state-administered.

The state agency reported initiatives in Milwaukee County. During the past year 6,000 children (2,500 families) received out-of-home care, and 450 children and 150 families received in-home services in Milwaukee County. The state projects that during the next year the number of children and families served in out-of-home care settings will remain the same, but the number served in-home will increase to 3,760 children and 1,250 families.

Milwaukee's child welfare service budget of $53 million for FY 98 came from state funds (77%), federal child welfare (20%), and substance abuse funds (3%). The project budget is $104 million for FY99.

To ensure quality in Milwaukee's child welfare system, the state agency uses reports from providers; standardized assessments; utilization, cost, and performance data from MIS tracking systems; monitoring staff; and program evaluations. The state tracks performance related to:

- Program effectiveness,
- The use of clinical protocols,
- Outcomes related to child functioning,
- Outcomes related to family functioning,
- Outcomes related to the achievement of the permanency plan goals, and
- Outcomes related to recidivism/reentry.

The Ongoing Case Management Program, the Safety Services Program, and Wraparound Milwaukee are the major initiatives underway in five geographically defined regions of the county. The RFP for ongoing case management services is fully described with brief profiles of the other two initiatives.

Milwaukee County Ongoing Case Management Program

In 1997, an RFP was released by the State Department of Health and Family Services, Division of Children and Family Services (DCFS) for ongoing case management and creation of treatment service networks by three lead agencies in Milwaukee County. Contracts were awarded to New Ventures, a Limited Liability Corporation (for Site 1 and Site 4), and Innovative Family Partnership (in Site 3). The county child welfare agency provides ongoing case management in Sites 2 and 5. Implementation began in January 1998. The RFP contained extensive descriptions of protocols and practice standards for the delivery of case management services and called for the contractor(s) to provide ongoing case management and create treatment service networks in three service sites. Contracts were entered with nonprofit, licensed child placing agencies functioning as "lead agencies," that provide or arrange for "ongoing case management" and services furnished through a network of neighborhood providers, and that are able to secure and coordinate reimbursement of Medical Assistance funding to support services not covered by the contract.

Goals. Central goals include improving the quality of services, increasing the safety and well-being of children, increasing permanency in the shortest time possible, and decreasing the length of stay in out-of-home care.

Populations Served. Children in Milwaukee County who have been maltreated or are at risk of maltreatment and their families (families define what constitutes "family" members for purposes of inclusion for case management) are eligible.

Case Management Responsibilities of the Lead Agency. According to the RFP, the lead agency will involve the extended family in the development of a safety plan. If the initial assessment determines that the child cannot remain safely at home, the child is placed and the child and family receive ongoing case management services, including:

- Reassessing child safety,

- Conducting a family assessment and developing a treatment plan,

- Developing an implementation plan to work toward reunification or other permanent home environment and reevaluation of the families progress toward goals,

- Arranging for the provision of services and coordinating care toward the achievement of treatment outcomes and permanency goals, and

- Ensuring safety plans for any children remaining in the home.

Placement Responsibilities of the Lead Agency. Responsibilities include taking the child into custody, seeking legal assistance and working with the social worker court liaison to file a petition, testifying in court, preparing court reports and any other court-related duties, taking responsibility for the out-of-home care plan for any placed child, and providing case management related to reunification before and after the child returns home or is adopted.

Responsibilities of State or County Agency. The state agency is responsible for the following functions: determination of Title IV-E eligibility, initial assessment and referral to lead agency, contracting with the lead agencies and contract monitoring, tracking outcomes and system performance indicators, claims payment, and the collection of data for the purpose of meeting state and federal reporting requirements. The county child welfare agency provides ongoing case management in two regions of the county and retains responsibility for foster care and adoption licensing and supervision.

Financial Arrangements. The DCFS budget includes funds from a variety of sources, including state funds, first and third party reimbursement, and Targeted Case Management funds available under Medicaid. According to the RFP, a total of $10,590,520 was available to make a maximum of three contract awards under the RFP (Site 1: $3,968,500; Site 4: $2,604,250; and $4,017,770 for Site 3).

The lead agency will collect and develop contractual arrangements with designated service providers who will collect first- and third-party reimbursement, including MA, and Targeted Case Management reimbursement for MA eligible children and families (thus, total funds cited do not include third-party reimbursement funds for these services).

For the first year, the lead agency will be reimbursed for 95% of the actual allowable costs reported on each month's expenditure report. The lead agency will receive an additional 5% if the lead agency meets the following requirements:

- For 90% of all new cases assigned, the Family Assessments and Treatment Plans are completed within 60 days of the assignment, and

- For 90% of the Treatment Plans completed for cases newly assigned, the Case Evaluation must be completed every 90 days following completion date of the treatment plan.

Reimbursement under these provisions will be on a cumulative basis (e.g., a lead agency not meeting the standards in the initial months of the contract but exceeding them subsequently may meet the total for the year and therefore meet the standards, the contractor receives the full 5%). For the second year, the lead agency is reimbursed 90% of actual allowable costs and an additional 5% for meeting the standards.

Additional reimbursement up to the full amount of reported costs is contingent upon the degree to which the lead agency achieves the cumulative percentage of permanent placements called for in the contract for new children assigned.

As part of the contract close-out process, there will be a reduction in reimbursement to 2% of the reported costs that can be earned for meeting the permanency targets, if the lead agency has more than a 30% recidivism rate in one year.

The lead agency will be eligible to receive additional payment based on its ability to reduce costs of out-of-home care. If the actual costs during the second year fall short of what has been projected, the DCFS intends to distribute a portion of the savings to the lead agencies. Those agencies achieving the greatest savings will receive the greatest return.

SafeNow Safety Services Program

The SafeNow Safety Services Program was initiated in January 1998, and uses a lead agency model to provide short-term intensive family preservation services for non-court involved families in Milwaukee County that have been identified as unsafe or at risk for maltreatment by a child protective services worker. The contract calls for the lead agencies to design and implement a two-year evaluation plan, subject to approval by the state agency.

Goals. Central goals include controlling for the safety of all of the children in the home; stabilizing and supporting the family through the development or enhancement of linkages with natural, formal, and informal supports; reaching an understanding of the causes of the safety concerns and facilitating the process of moving the family toward self-management of the child safety issues; and preventing the unnecessary out-of-home placement of children.

Populations Served. Children and families who have been identified as unsafe or at risk of maltreatment by a child protective service worker are eligible for inclusion in this initiative.

During the past year, 1,062 children and 354 families received services from this initiative. The county projects 3,378 children and 1,126 families will receive services during the upcoming year.

Services. This initiative includes the delivery of short-term intensive family preservation services.

Quality and Outcomes. The state will monitor quality requirements and outcome measures in the following areas:

- Specific system performance indicators related to program effectiveness,
- Specific criteria related to cost,
- Specific criteria related to access/availability of services and utilization patterns (18 core services are required, no waiting lists are permitted, and utilization is reviewed monthly),
- Specific criteria related to appropriateness of services,
- Consumer satisfaction requirement (consumer satisfaction surveys are required at case closure),

- Outcomes related to child functioning are being developed,
- Outcomes related to family functioning (evaluation of the number of case closures due to achievement of family managed safety plan),
- Outcomes related to recidivism/reentry will be instituted,
- Requirements to adhere to professional standards or licensing requirements, and
- Specific criteria or standards related to cultural competence of providers.

Roles and Responsibilities. Four lead agencies were selected. In addition to the county agency and the two not-for-profit service delivery networks (New Ventures and Innovative Family Partnership), the other lead agency is a new entity created by a behavioral health managed care company (Magellan Public Solutions) and two nonprofit community-based agencies.

The state child welfare agency will have primary responsibility for creating medical necessity or service necessity criteria and for tracking outcome and system performance indicators.

The lead agencies operating under a risk-share contract will have primary responsibility for the following functions: preauthorizing care, gatekeeping for certain care, ongoing utilization management, contracting with providers, creating provider networks, case management services, billing and reimbursement, and the collection of data for the purpose of meeting state and federal reporting requirements.

Financial Arrangements. This initiative plans to share risk with service providers, but has not yet determined the risk-sharing arrangement. Funding of $3,447,074 was used to support this initiative during the past year, $6,286,940 has been allocated for the upcoming year. The child welfare agency contributes the majority (93%) of the funding and Medicaid provides the remainder (7%).

Wraparound Milwaukee

According to the recent GAO report, the publicly managed Wraparound Milwaukee program, initiated in June 1996, provides wraparound services for Children with SED at risk of residential placement. It served 600 children during 1998. The program blends Medicaid, child welfare, and federal grant funds into a single buying pool to purchase individualized, family-based services to help children at risk of placement or placed in residential treatment centers return to their family, foster family, or other living arrangement in the community.

The county child welfare agency agreed to pay a monthly case rate of $3,300 per child out of its institutional placement budget. The state health care financing agency contributes a monthly case rate of $1,459 (included in the $3,300 rate) to pay for all mental health and substance abuse services for Medicaid-eligible children, who make up about 80% of the program's population. Along with a federal grant from the Center for Mental Health Services, these child welfare and Medicaid dollars form the funding pool from which the public managed care entity pays the cost of residential treatment, group and foster care, and all other services, except physical health care, which is outside the contract.

The Wraparound Program has reduced the number of children in residential treatment, and, as a result, state and local costs are almost 40% less per child than under the previous system. Moreover, the program's Mobile Crisis Team's gatekeeping functions and development of treatment plans have resulted in a 55% reduction in inpatient hospital days, as well as nearly 200 fewer children in need of residential care between 1994 and 1997. Furthermore, reinvestment from these savings has enabled the project to serve 44% more children with the same money.

Note: The state agency did not specifically describe any of the three Milwaukee initiatives. The state did provide budget figures and described the state's role in managing Milwaukee's child welfare services and provided information on the numbers of children and families receiving services in Milwaukee's programs. The Case Management Program description is based on the RFP and the other two initiatives were described in the October 1998 GAO report, *Child Welfare: Early Experiences Implementing a Managed Care Approach*. The GAO report is based on a survey conducted in March 1998. Additionally, the Director of SafeNow Safety Services provided detailed information to the Managed Care Institute.

FOR MORE INFORMATION
Contacts for Initiatives

STATE/COUNTY	INITIATIVE	RESPONDENT	PHONE
Arizona	Family Builders	Anna Arnold	602/542-3714
Arizona	Privatization Service Delivery	Wendy Bergsman	602/542-5678
California	Senate Bill 163-Wraparound Services	Kay Ryan	916/445-2875
California – San Diego Co.	Project Heartbeat	Rey Galindo	619/231-0781
Colorado – El Paso County	Child Protection System & Pikes Peak OPTIONS Behavioral Health	David Berns	719/444-5532
Connecticut	Continuum of Care	Eileen Breslin	860/550-6349
Delaware	Low Risk Treatment	Janet Spina	302/633-2657
Florida	Privatization Pilots	Theresa Leslie	850/922-3937
Georgia	(MATCH) Multi-Agency Team for Children	Diane Sacks	404/657-3578
Hawaii	Ohana Family Conferencing	John Walters	808/586-5667
Illinois	Performance Contracting	Mike Shaver	312/814-8740
Indiana	Title IV-E Foster Care Waiver	Cathleen Graham	317/232-4423
Kansas	Privatization of Adoption, Foster Care, and Family Preservation	Marilyn Jacobson	785/296-4653
Kentucky	Quality Care Pilot	Pat Wilson	502/564-3703
Maryland -Baltimore City	Child Welfare Managed Care Pilot	Deanna Phelps	410/361-2127
Massachusetts	Commonworks	Robert Wentworth	617/727-3171
Massachusetts	Family Based Services	Ben Lessing	617/727-3171
Michigan	Michigan's Families (Title IV-E waiver demonstration)	Lizbeth Leeson	616/691-8851
Minnesota – Hennepin Co.	Children's Mental Health Collaborative	Veronica Schulz	612/348-3535
Missouri	Interdepartmental Initiative for Children with Severe Needs	Lisa Clements	573/751-8215
New York	Neighborhood-Based Services Initiative (The Bronx)	Elan Melamid	212/266-2906

151

North Carolina – Buncombe Co.	Title IV-E waiver demonstration	Mandy Stone	828/255-5749
Ohio – Crawford County	Children's Services	Jeff Swearingen	419/468-3255
Ohio – Cuyahoga County	Managed Care Initiative	Jim McCafferty	216/432-3395
Ohio – Franklin County	Managed Care Contracting	Sharon Watkins	614/275-2571
Ohio – Hamilton County	Behavioral Health Services & Creative Connections	Lora Neltner	513/946-2132
Ohio – Lorain County	Integrated Services Partnership	Sue Nowlin	440/329-5339
Oklahoma	Children's Services	Catalina Herrerias	402/522-0331
Pennsylvania – Berk County	Berkserve	George Kovarie	610/478-6725
South Carolina	Adoption Services	Marcus D. Mann	803/734-5972
Tennessee	Nonresidential Networks & Continuum of Care Contracts	Lisa Faehl	615/741-8905
Texas	(PACE) Permanency Achieved through Coordinated Efforts	Cindy Bourland	512/438-4462
Utah	Residential Contract Restructuring	Zoherh Saunder	801/538-4623
Washington	Capitated Payment for Children with Special Needs (Title IV-E waiver demonstration)	Phil Bayne	360/902-7911
West Virginia	Region IV Foster Care Pilot Project	Thomas Strawderman	304/558-7980
Wisconsin	SafeNow Safety Services & Milwaukee County Case Management	Linda Bichler	414/257-8072

CWLA Contacts

Charlotte McCullough
Director, Managed Care Institue & AAPCS Child Mental Health Division
202/942-0242 • cmccullo@cwla.org

Barbara Schmitt
Associate Director, Managed Care Institute
202/942-0246 • bschmitt@cwla.org

Child Welfare League of America
440 First Street NW, Third Floor
Washington, DC 20001-2085

REFERENCES

Schulzinger, R., McCarthy, J., Meyers, J., de la Cruz Irvine, M., & Vincent, P. (February 1999). *Health care reform tracking project: Tracking state managed care reforms as they affect children and adolescents with behavioral health disorders and their families. Special analysis: Child welfare managed care reform initiative* (The 1997/98 state survey). Washington, DC: National Technical Assistance Center for Children's Mental Health.

U.S. Government Accounting Office [GAO]. (October 21, 1998). *Child welfare: Early experiences implementing a managed care approach.* GAO Report GAO/HEHS-998. Washington, DC: Author.

Wehr, E., Valencia, R., Shaw, K., & Rosenbaum, S. (1998). *Interim findings from an analysis of risk-based purchasing agreements for child protective services* [DRAFT]. Washington, DC: Center for Health Policy Research at the George Washington University Medical Center.